200
PROJECTS
TO GET YOU INTO
FASHION
DESIGN

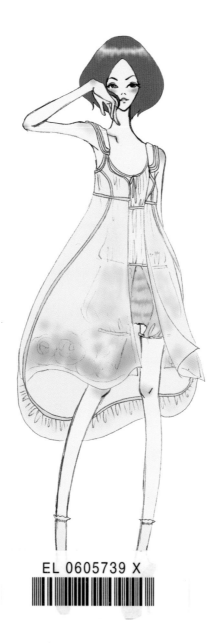

200
PROJECTS
TO GET YOU INTO
FASHION
DESIGN

Tracy Fitzgerald and Adrian Grandon

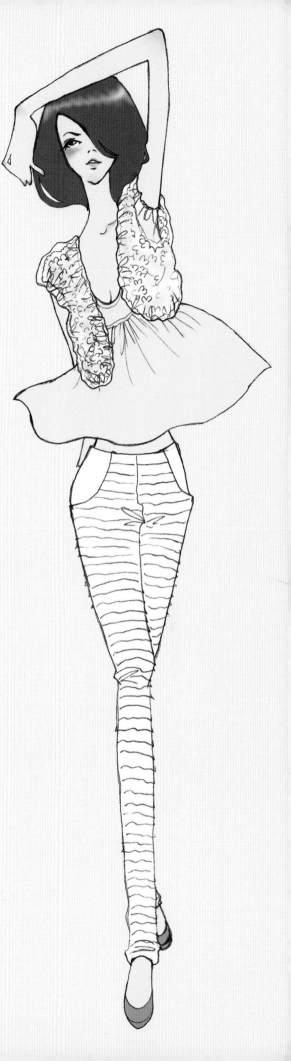

A QUARTO BOOK

Published in 2009 by
A&C Black Publishers
36 Soho Square
London W1D 3QY
www.acblack.com

Reprinted 2010(twice)

ISBN: 978-14081-0825-3

A CIP record for this book is available from the British Library.

QUAR.WGFD

Conceived, designed and produced by
Quarto Publishing plc
The Old Brewery
6 Blundell Street
London N7 9BH

Senior editor: Letitia Luff
Copy editors: Claire Waite Brown and Diana Craig
Art director: Caroline Guest
Art editor: Emma Clayton
Designer: Karin Skånberg
Photographer: Martin Norris

Creative director: Moira Clinch
Publisher: Paul Carslake

Color separation by PICA Digital Pte Ltd, Singapore
Printed in Singapore by Star Standard (Pte) Ltd

9 8 7 6 5 4 3

Contents

Foreword

You are about to join an elite band of people who know what fashion is and understand how it comes together. Welcome to the world of fashion.

This book will give you advice on how to take your interest in fashion further than just shopping or reading magazines. Only a few of the young designers who apply to study fashion are accepted by the fashion school of their choice every year. If you complete the projects in this book you will maximize your chance of success in this competitive field based on the experience that we have acquired through years spent working in the industry and in fashion education. Effectively a fashion school in a book, it will prepare you to achieve your goal by challenging your fashion sense, inspiring your thinking, and developing your skills. Solid research, drawing, and designing lie at the heart of the book – these drive originality and creativity. The themes and projects will be of interest to fashion school aspirants, and useful for educators.

When you are doing your work, and fashion is hard work, make sure you enjoy it. The most important thing to remember is that fashion is fast-moving, inspiring, exciting, and glamorous, and most of all should be fun.

Tracy Fitzgerald and Adrian Grandon
Fashion/Textile Design
University of the West of England

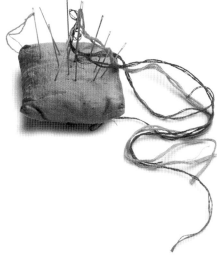

GET STARTED IN FASHION
Research, design and drawing, attention to detail, and an eye for presentation are essential for students of fashion. This book will build your skills in these areas and more.

About this book

Although completing the workouts in this book might not guarantee your admission into fashion school, it will give you a good fighting chance. Learn to create fashion that reflects your understanding of basic design principles, shows your versatility using a variety of media, and gives you the necessary motivation to produce a memorable collection of garment designs in your own style.

THE FIRST FOUR CHAPTERS (PAGES 8–107)

As a designer your most important asset is to be able to think through a project. It is this skill that will impress interviewers at college or in industry. This book takes you through the design process, from primary research and getting your first ideas, through their development in 2D and then in 3D, to making and promoting your finished collection. You can do all the workouts if you wish, or select just a few in areas that interest you, but you will get the most from them if you work through the book from front to back.

THE SEWING CHAPTER (PAGES 108–119)

As a fashion designer you need to be able to make garments, so some basic techniques are explained in the sewing chapter. You may want to refer to it as you work through the rest of the book, or work through the exercises one by one.

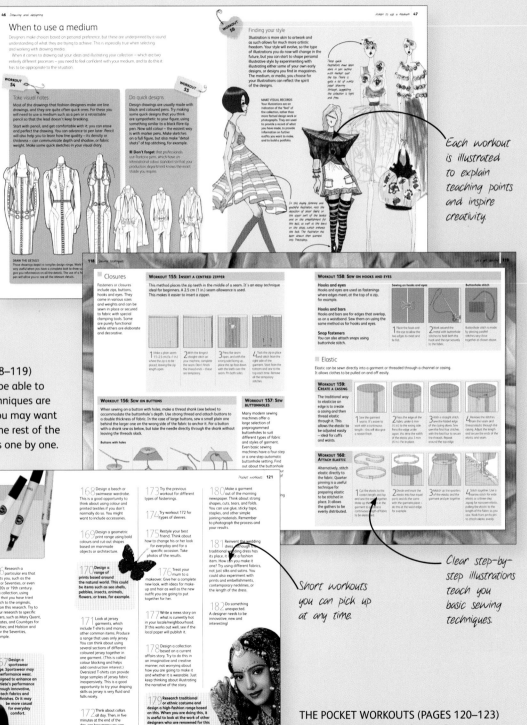

Each workout is illustrated to explain teaching points and inspire creativity.

Clear step-by-step illustrations teach you basic sewing techniques.

Short workouts you can pick up at any time.

THE POCKET WORKOUTS (PAGES 120–123)

Dip into this collection of quick-fire workouts at any time to practise new skills, or discover a new area of fashion design.

Chapter one:
Getting started

These workouts form the first steps of your fashion career. You will begin to learn how fashion works, from measuring figures to thinking about garments, from choosing a sketchbook to basic print work. They will give you research skills in fashion and, most importantly, inspire you.

What you need

In order to complete the workouts in this book you will need to assemble the necessary equipment. Much of this equipment will be available at your school or college. When purchasing equipment, remember that the quality and appropriateness of your materials is paramount.

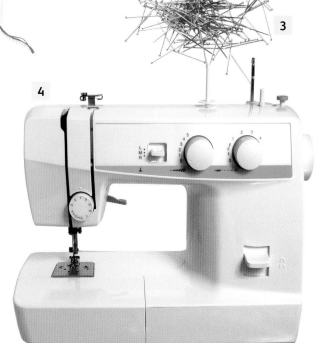

1 Needles and coloured threads.

2 Tape measure.

3 Dressmaker's pins.

4 Sewing machine. You get what you pay for so you might want to use the machines at your school or college when you first start out.

5 Dress stand. The adjustable blue dress stand is an ideal model to start with. The dimensions can be easily adjusted to match your own or a friend's. The solid, linen-covered Kennet and Lindsell dress stand in a sample size 8 is the fashion industry standard. The clear seam lines help to achieve accurate pattern cutting, but it is only available in standard dress sizes and isn't adjustable.

6 Scissors. You might want two pairs and to keep one pair only for cutting fabric.

7 Tailor's chalk. This is ideal for marking fabric for cutting and can be brushed away easily.

8 Sketchbook. Workout 1 gives you more information about finding a sketchbook.

9 Eraser.

10 Coloured pencils.

11 A variety of media with which to add colour. For example, gouache paints and marker pens.

12 Craft knife.

13 Graphite pencils and drawing pens.

14 Computer. Many designers draw with a design package or scan in their sketches and add colour and textural finishes. Apple computers (Macs) are favoured by many designers. You might want to use the machines at your school or college when you first start out.

15 French curves and rulers. A 5 x 45 cm (2 x 18 in.) clear ruler with a 0.5 cm (¹⁄₁₆ in.) grid is especially useful.

16 Plain cotton fabric. For example, calico or sheeting.

17 Iron and ironing board.

18 Paper. A range of different weights and textures of paper are useful.

19 Digital camera. Essential for taking visual research notes, documenting your designs, and taking to your first fashion shoots. Choose a small, light model and keep it with you.

Choosing a sketchbook

Your first task is to find a suitable sketchbook. The sketchbook is the designer's "bible". You need to think of it as a repository for all your ideas and use it to start developing your own way of working. The most important aspect of a sketchbook is that it serves as a basis for research: it will house visual information you have gathered and relevant notes and analysis. Sketchbooks are available in many different formats: landscape, portrait, spiral bound, decorative, functional. There are also those with textured and coloured papers. Most importantly, always try and go for the best quality paper you are able to afford.

See also

GET INSPIRED,
PAGE 14

GET OUT THERE,
PAGE 15

WORKOUT 1

Decide on size

Choose your first sketchbook based on size – it can be just about any format you prefer. Sketchbooks come in various sizes ranging from small ones about 89 x 140 mm (3½ x 5½ in.), which are convenient to carry in your back pocket; mid-sized ones about 216 x 279 mm (8½ x 11 in.); or large books about 420 x 594 mm (16½ x 23½ in.), which are big enough to enable you to develop several ideas on the page, but are not easily portable.

Later, once you discover your favourite sketching medium, you can choose sketchbooks with appropriate paper. If you often use gouache paint, for example, the sturdier paper is better. For marker pens, a slicker paper is best so that you can illustrate in a more gestural way and the paper won't absorb the pigment as fast.

START YOUR COLLECTION
Usually you will find you have several sketchbooks on the go at the same time, but the one you use every day will be the one that you can carry around with you. This sketchbook should travel with you everywhere. It is the place to record ideas, sites that interest you, and fashion that excites you. The larger sketchbooks are ideal for working out ideas regarding your own projects and for collecting images.

Personalize your sketchbook

Your sketchbook is going to make an individual statement about you and your ideas, so start by making it personal. Gather a collection of materials that are special to you, such as photographs of friends and family, or postcards of places you have enjoyed visiting, and stick these into the book alongside any other mementos. Consider the sketchbook as your "world" that represents you non-verbally through images, fabric, design work, and anything else you choose to include. Even the way you write should evoke your aesthetic and vision.

■ **Don't forget** to write your name and contact details in the front of the book in case you lose it.

REVEAL YOURSELF
Like the owner of this sketchbook, you could paste photographs of yourself and your family, from the past to present, along with notes of likes and dislikes, into your book. Someone should be able to begin to build up an idea of your personality by looking at your sketchbook.

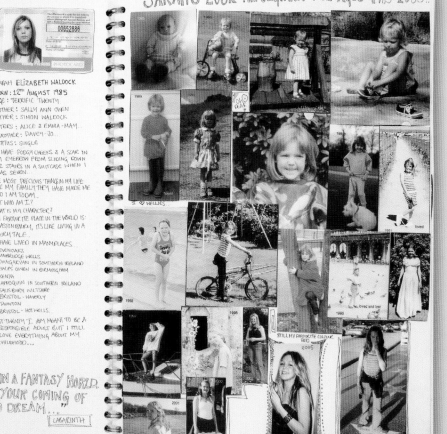

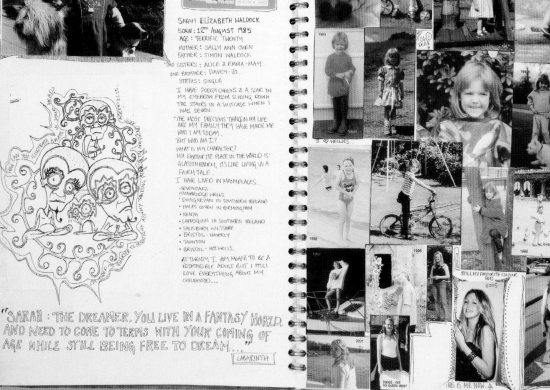

Doing research

Research is the foundation of all of your original design work. The broader your research the more interesting and innovative your own designs will be. By carrying out thorough research, you will make exciting discoveries that will support your own new ideas.

Research is divided into two distinct types, primary and secondary. Primary research means that you have looked directly at the original source and worked from it, for example by drawing people you have met, making sketches of historical costumes in a museum, or taking photographs of garments, people, landscapes, or objects.

Secondary research means that you have worked from already existing imagery that has been produced by other practitioners, for example by looking at magazines and posters, or watching films and television programmes.

Many research tasks may not seem related to fashion at all, but you will inevitably find that you continue to draw on the themes you study throughout your career, particularly if they include other aspects of design. Good research will also back up the other skills you need to be successful in your career as a fashion designer.

WORKOUT 3

Begin primary research

Now that you have personalized your sketchbook, the first blank page should not look too daunting. Start your primary research by drawing things that have some meaning to you, perhaps objects from your home or bedroom, or your pet. You can take as much or as little time with each drawing as you see fit. You may also choose to draw only a small aspect of the object, rather than the whole thing.

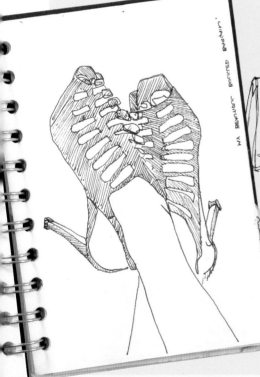

USE YOUR SPARE TIME
Sketch whenever you have a spare minute, starting with the things around you, for example, your shoes and handbags.

WORKOUT 4

Get inspired

If you have your own workspace at home, or at school or college, then you can set it up to inspire you. This is like an extension of your sketchbook and should include all your favourite things but in 3D.

MAKE A STATEMENT
Here is a good example of a workspace or station, personalized with the designer's current influences of Victoriana and artefacts relating to taxidermy.

WORKOUT 5

Develop your fashion eye

Take photographs of interesting people, starting with friends or colleagues to give you confidence. From this point progress to more challenging subjects, for example, a small, up-and-coming band, kids at the local skate park, or other subcultures. Fashion designers need to be able to identify and respond to new trends, particularly in streetwear. You will also develop an idea of the sort of person you wish to design for – your customer or muse. Camera phones and compact digital cameras are an easy and quick way to obtain reference and styling information.

BE ON THE LOOKOUT
These photos show individual fashion statements spotted on a walk around the city centre. Always ask permission before photographing people – when you tell them why they will often be happy to pose for you.

Contrasting strong colours make a confident statement.

This is an unusual combination of big woolly hat and sparkly backless top.

Cheap, fun accessories personalize this look.

WORKOUT 6

Get out there

Start drawing all the time. The most fertile areas for ideas are museums, costume and fashion history, architecture, forms in nature – whatever interests you. Sketch anything that catches your eye; it doesn't have to be fashion related. You can translate it later into motif, texture, colour, detail, and silhouette.

LEARN FROM NATURE
To be a good designer, you need to be a versatile sketcher. The work shown here is based around the study of flowers and has been carried out in a variety of media, including pencil and watercolour.

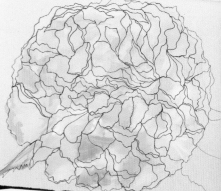

WORKOUT 7

Begin secondary research

Add some secondary research to your sketchbook. Tear out images from newspapers and magazines – they could be purely visual or relate to songs, films, books, or poems – that can be used together to illustrate relationships and juxtapositions. Pick your favourite grouping and make drawings or invent some imagery based on it.

STUDY THE STARS

Classic and contemporary films also provide good reference material. Vintage Hollywood starlets ooze glamour and period detail. The costume of Captain Sparrow from *Pirates of the Caribbean*, while not strictly true to an era, displays an exciting and flamboyant look that can be adapted for fashion.

DELVE INTO CHILDHOOD MEMORIES

The pages from this sketchbook show varied imagery relating to children's stories and films, such as *The Chronicles of Narnia*, circuses, and the designer's personal childhood memories.

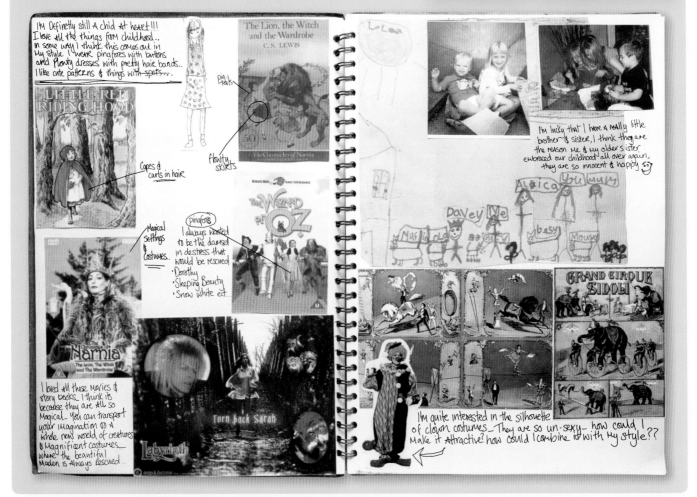

Edit your research

From the large amount of research you have undertaken, print out or photocopy some of your favourite imagery, cut it out neatly, and paste it onto a single board. This is called the mood board or theme board. Remember that you can't use everything so edit down your research to avoid it being redundant. Your mood boards should give you a strong sense of colour, silhouette, "gesture", and feeling. It is your most important reference tool and you will be referring back to it constantly throughout the design process.

This board conveys a strong sense of the atmosphere and evocative silhouettes of the ballet.

This carnival imagery is excellent reference for colour, texture, and embellishment.

GET IN THE MOOD
A mood board can consist of any number of images but usually is distilled down to just three or four really strong elements. Feel free to mix and match photographic and fine art imagery as shown on the ballet mood board (above).

Visualize

Learning to visualize imagery is the most important step on the way to strong design development. You need to begin to turn the images you have collected into fashion ideas. Start now by taking one of your favourite images and experiment by creating texture or pattern from it.

LOOK FOR PATTERN
The image of the mistletoe (above) has been translated into a simple pattern that could be used as a starting point for ideas about print and colour.

THINK ABOUT FORM
You can also explore designs in three dimensions. Here the designer has used paper folding to help visualize design elements of this orchid (left) in 3D and how they could be translated to the body.

Thinking about fashion

Fashion is obviously about clothes, and research into older and current garments is invaluable to a fashion designer. One of the best sources of reference is an old or vintage garment, so search carefully through garage sales, second-hand shops, flea markets, and relatives' wardrobes and make notes on garments from different eras.

See also
BEGIN SECONDARY RESEARCH,
PAGE 16

WORKOUT 10

Identify period style

Pick out a selection of garments from a vintage store and try to work out which era they come from. Buy one garment to use for further research. Research the era you think the garment comes from on the Internet or at the library, and compare it with the images you find. Try looking at www.vintagefashionguild.org as a starting point. Don't worry if you can't match the garments exactly to a date, as long as you get an understanding of the important silhouettes, details, and fabrics used at the time.

LOOK FOR PERIOD CLUES
The shape and lace trim on the garment (left) identifies it as underwear from the turn of the 20th century. The bodice (below) is homemade and so harder to date, but the colour and style suggest early 1960s.

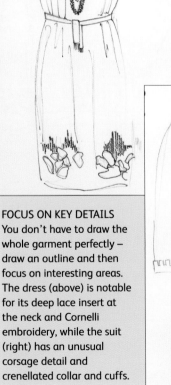

WORKOUT 11

Draw the garment

Consider what it is about the garment that interests you. First think about it as a whole. Lay it out flat in front of you and draw it in your sketchbook. The easiest way to do this is to start at the centre top – usually around the neck – and work out and down.

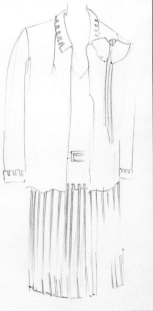

FOCUS ON KEY DETAILS
You don't have to draw the whole garment perfectly – draw an outline and then focus on interesting areas. The dress (above) is notable for its deep lace insert at the neck and Cornelli embroidery, while the suit (right) has an unusual corsage detail and crenellated collar and cuffs.

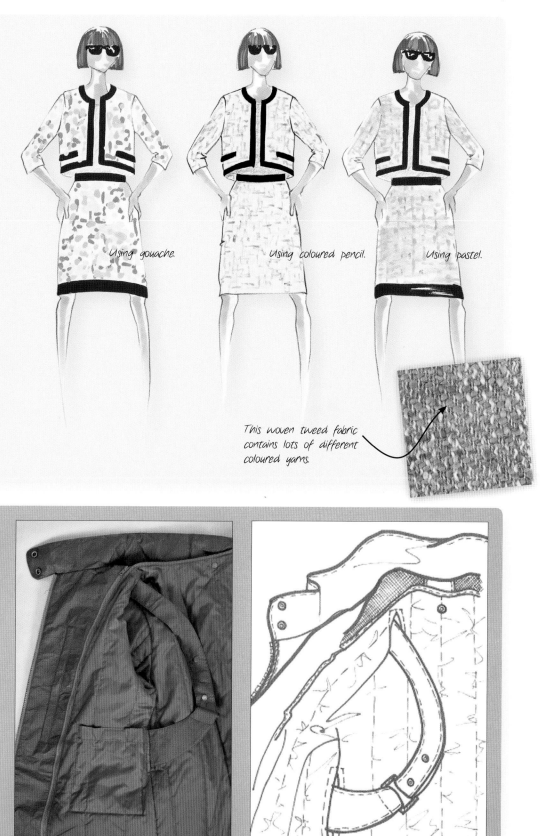

WORKOUT 12

Add colour

At this point you should also indicate the colour of the fabric your vintage garment is made from. Using your preferred colour medium, try mixing the colour next to your drawing. When you have achieved the right shade, apply it to your drawing.

SUGGEST PATTERN

If you want to show small-scale patterns, such as this vintage tweed fabric, don't get too involved in the rendering; it should give a sense of scale and colour relationships. To get the scale of a pattern correct, relate it to your eye, then relate it to your figure's eye and render to that scale.

Using gouache.

Using coloured pencil.

Using pastel.

This woven tweed fabric contains lots of different coloured yarns.

WORKOUT 13

Study the detail

Identify any interesting details of the garment and draw these in your sketchbook. These could be elements that you don't normally see on contemporary clothes, or anything that is new or looks different to you. You will have to use your discretion here – what's commonplace for one person may be rarely seen by another.

LOOK INSIDE AND OUT

Interesting detail can be found anywhere on a garment. It was details of the construction of this old coat, rather than its external appearance, that caught the designer's eye.

Ethical fashion

Because of the impact that the manufacture of fashion items and related products have on the wider world, it is important to consider the ethics of your work. When you research fair-trade and organically produced fabrics and other materials, you will find that there is a strong international movement in this field, including famous labels such as Stella McCartney and American Apparel.

Quite often fair-trade or greener garments are not design-led, but as a fashion designer it is important that your products are, so you will need to make an extra effort to ensure that the two work well together.

WORKOUT 14

Use ethical materials

Try to find examples of ethically produced fabrics on the Internet. Bear in mind that many of these come in neutral colours and that this may limit your colour palette. Here, this collection made with ethical fabrics creates a highly feminine feel by cleverly using details such as a picot edge, satin bows, and floral prints.

This is hemp fabric (mixed with Tencel®) with an organic cotton lace trim.

This leopard print jersey fabric is made from bamboo fibres.

KNOW YOUR SOURCES
There are various criteria that garments must meet in order to be labelled "ethical". They need to be made from sustainably produced fabrics and accessories, using environmentally friendly processes. A fair wage must also be paid to workers constructing the garments and the work carried out in safe and appropriate surroundings.

Research a label

Look at a fashion label that has had bad press in the past about its ethical record, whether through its relationship with factories with poor labour conditions or through ecological damage it has caused to the environment. What steps did the label take to clean up its act?

Here the hemp and Tencel® fabric is matched with a decorative trim reclaimed from vintage garments.

Reuse, reduce, recycle

Spend three months not buying any brand-new clothes, while also wearing a new outfit every day. Not only will this test your imagination, but hopefully will also bring you to a more innovative way of dressing. Accessorize what you are wearing and put outfits together differently. Within this task you can buy vintage or second-hand items, so try mixing vintage and contemporary garments.

Keep a record of what you wear each day so that you can check how your "look" is developing and whether you are repeating too many outfit ideas.

■ **Don't forget** that dressing unconventionally and looking different is how cutting-edge fashion thrives.

RECORD YOUR OUTFITS
Take a photo of your reused and recycled outfits every morning. Use the timer on your digital camera, or you can take pictures of yourself in the mirror.

Taking notes

There are many different styles of drawing, but the collecting of information for fashion design requires a clear and informative type of drawing. You need to develop a professional approach to taking notes. Now that you have started drawing, see if you can show the full range of details that a designer would be expected to look at.

See also
GET OUT THERE,
PAGE 15

WORKOUT 17

Do a detailed drawing: right side

Lay a garment out in front of you, ready to be drawn. Make sure it is completely flat. Your drawing needs to start at the centre front, and especially needs to be in proportion. Make a complete drawing with stitching, seams, darts, buttons, and fastenings all indicated. You can use the information you gather to inform you about how you should make up your own garments in the future.

■ **Don't forget** you can draw a line down the centre of your page and use this as the centre of the front of your garment.

FIND THE INTERESTING DETAILS
This men's jacket in cotton has a simple rectangle shape. The interest lies in the detail of the collar and pockets and how it has been stitched together.

WORKOUT 18

Do a detailed drawing: wrong side

Turn a garment inside out and draw it in a similar way to that shown for the right side in the previous workout. Pay particular attention to the finish of seams and other elements, such as how the pockets have been made, and any linings or facings. Also check the back for interesting details.

LOOK INSIDE
The inside of a garment can reveal its construction. Try drawing this jacket, showing the construction on the back and the patch pocket with flap on the chest. Indicate the loose facing in a shaded tone.

Experiment with styles

Choose a single garment and try drawing it using several different techniques and media, to discover how such choices affect the appearance of the final image. It will also help you understand which media to choose when drawing particular types of garments and fabrics.

Flat marker emphasizes the silhouette.

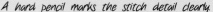

A hard pencil marks the stitch detail clearly.

A continuous pen line shows basic construction in an interesting way.

Pencil shading indicates the soft texture of the vintage leather.

CREATE DIFFERENT EFFECTS
This 1980s grey leather jacket has been drawn in four different ways, each technique highlighting a different aspect of the garment.

Start a visual diary

One of the most important considerations for someone who works in the field of fashion is to have an understanding of the human body. Now that you have started to look at clothing you should also start researching people. Use your sketchbook – or if it is too big have a separate book that will fit into your pocket or bag – as a "visual diary" in which you draw friends or any "interesting" people you see and who may inspire future designs. It doesn't matter what the person looks like. Young or old, male or female, all are good – in fact the more diverse the visual diary becomes the better.

Try different approaches, for example make outline or tonal drawings, or draw the negative space that surrounds the figure. Also vary the time you take, doing sketches for, say, 30 seconds, or drawings for up to an hour. Using the opposite hand to your normal drawing hand will make your drawings freer.

■ **Don't forget** to get used to carrying your visual diary with you at all times and aim to make a drawing a day. If you can't find anyone interesting to draw, make a sketch of a still life or landscape instead.

MAKE QUICK SKETCHES
This sketch shows lots of movement using a layering effect – wax crayon over pencil.

Measuring up

To make things easier in fashion design and manufacture, body and garment measurements have been standardized. However, to confuse everyone, the standards vary from country to country and between manufacturers.

WORKOUT
21

Categorize body shapes

It is now generally agreed that there are many types of female figure. When you look at people, ascertain which category you think they fit into and think about whether their clothing style does – or does not – suit their shape.

ALL DIFFERENT SIZES
There are so many figure variations that they are too numerous to list. Here are some general shapes you can start to think about.

Narrow rectangle   Hourglass   Bottom-heavy triangle   Top-heavy triangle   Circle   Oval

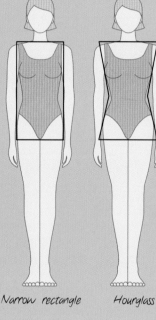

Measure the body

Try measuring a friend, or ask a friend to measure you, using a measuring tape. You need to remove your outer garments to ensure the measurements are exact. Using the diagrams on the right, take measurements of all the different points indicated on the body.

GET THE RIGHT FIT
Before making or buying a pattern to sew, check the necessary measurements against those of the person you are sewing it for and make any adjustments to the pattern before you begin.

WORKOUT
22

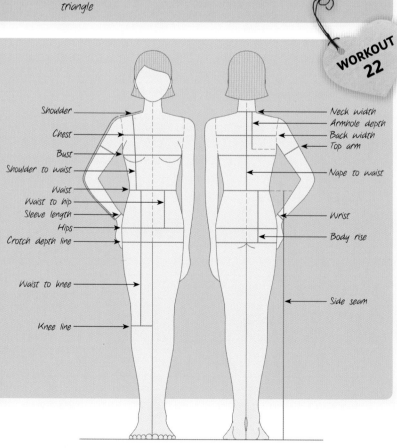

Shoulder
Chest
Bust
Shoulder to waist
Waist
Waist to hip
Sleeve length
Hips
Crotch depth line
Waist to knee
Knee line

Neck width
Armhole depth
Back width
Top arm
Nape to waist
Wrist
Body rise
Side seam

Measure clothes

It is useful to be able to take accurate measurements of a garment so you can recreate pieces that you like. This exercise is called "spec-ing" in the fashion industry. Using the information below as a guide, take measurements of a coat to practise your technique.

NOTE THE MEASUREMENTS

This working drawing (below) shows a detailed front view of a trench coat. The key measurements are the chest, waist, hip, shoulder, and sleeve length, alongside armhole depth and neck width. Obviously, the more measurements you include the more accurate the translation into a finished garment.

KEEP IT FLAT

All measurements are taken with the garment flat. For example, you measure across the front of the waistband (above left). The back of the waistband is a separate measurement. You also need to take time to arrange the shoulder seams and collar so you can measure accurately from the correct point (above).

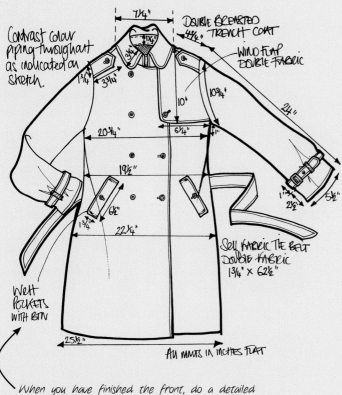

Contrast colour piping throughout as indicated on sketch.

DOUBLE BREASTED TRENCH COAT

WIND FLAP DOUBLE FABRIC

7¼"
4¼"
3¼"
1¾"
3¾"
10"
10¾"
24"
20¾"
6¼"
4"
19½"
1"
2½"
5½"
6½"
1¾"
22¼"

Self fabric tie belt double fabric
1¾" × 62½"

Welt pockets with btn

25½"

ALL MMTS IN INCHES FLAT

When you have finished the front, do a detailed drawing of the back of the coat too.

Master measuring

To get used to the measuring process, try taking the measurements of a number of different garments, such as skirts and trousers, knitwear, and different types of dresses.

Analyzing a collection

Up until this point we have been looking at individual items of clothing in detail. We are now going to look at garments in the context of a collection. A collection is the work of one design studio that is specific to just one season and has a visual vocabulary that is repeated throughout a range of garments. It is where the designer will show their new ideas as well as incorporate some of their signature details, shapes, and fabrics.

See also

DEVELOP YOUR FASHION EYE,
PAGE 15

BEGIN SECONDARY RESEARCH,
PAGE 16

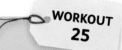

Describe collections

WORKOUT 25

Look at the Christian Dior autumn/winter 2008 collection. The silhouette shows nipped-in waists and full, often circular skirts, which were hallmarks of 1950s fashion. Look at the colours used and other details. The description could be "Fifties-inspired, pastel-coloured, layered transparency".

Compare this to Gareth Pugh's autumn/winter 2008 collection, which is futuristic with an undercurrent of gothic. The colours are greys and blacks and the fabrics are edgy. The description could be "techno, future, goth – menswear inspired by the god Pan".

Study different designers' collections by logging onto www.style.com/vogue or www.fashion.net, which provide free access to the latest runway shows. Describe the look of each collection.

Identify common themes

WORKOUT 26

When you research a collection, try to identify where designers have used the same colours and fabrics, where the shape of the garment has been repeated, and where details such as collars, ties and fastenings, and finishings have been repeated. Look at the collection below by Etienne Ozeki. You will notice that the overall "feel" of the collection is youthful and very casual in appearance. Within the various items you should also be able to pick out certain similarities.

- Denim is used throughout as a highlight or accent detail, especially around pockets, where you would expect to see it, and collars.

- A strong military influence can be seen in the use of camouflage and colour palette.

- The whole collection has been industrially stone-washed to give the "worn" appearance.

LOOK FOR SIMILARITIES
This Etienne Ozeki "look book" shows the full range of ideas across a collection.

See the similarities

Look again at the Etienne Ozeki collection shown in workout 25 and see if you can identify five more similarities. You could start by thinking about fabrics, shapes, influences, and branding, for example. What other similarities can you see?

Identify the wearer

Collections may consist of a small number of separates, as shown in the "look book" opposite, or be huge collections of many different looks for all occasions. Look at the Gucci collection below and try to work out who it is aimed at. Make a "customer board" about the typical person who wears Gucci clothes. A customer board is similar to a mood board (see workout 8) and uses one or more images to explain who the customer is without using any text at all.

WHO WEARS GUCCI?
A vintage Gucci collection showing several womenswear looks, some more appropriate for day wear, some definitely for evening wear.

Exploring silhouette

Silhouette is the shape a garment makes when worn. It can also be applied to flat garments. It is an important element to take into consideration when designing a collection or when buying clothes.

Study silhouettes

Look at the silhouettes below and try to find them in your wardrobe or in a store. Look at how details have been added, and colour used, to enhance the silhouette. Take visual notes in your sketchbook.

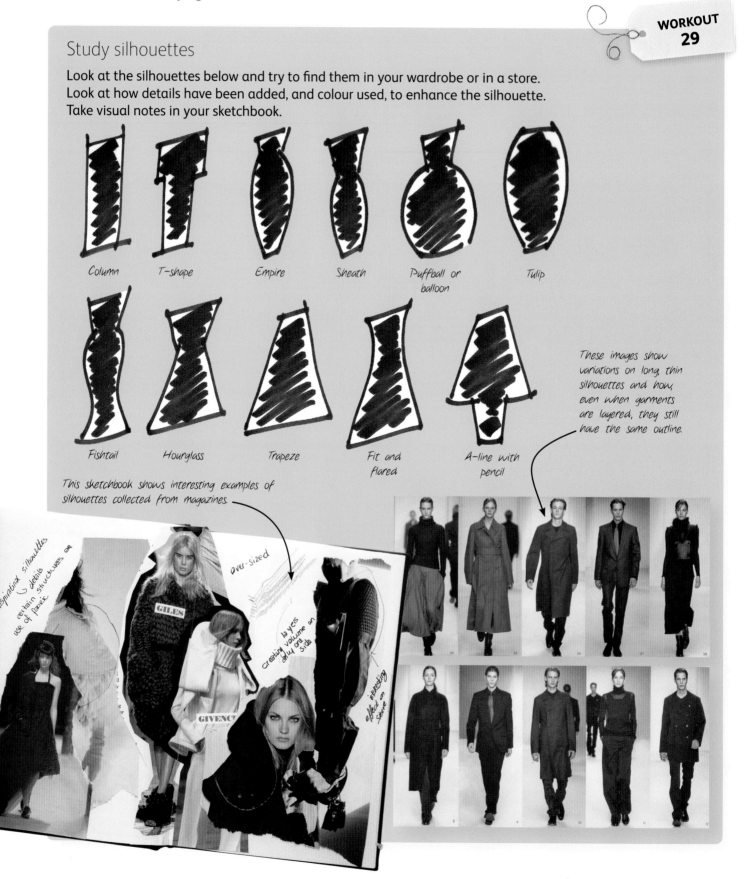

Column   T-shape   Empire   Sheath   Puffball or balloon   Tulip

Fishtail   Hourglass   Trapeze   Fit and flared   A-line with pencil

These images show variations on long, thin silhouettes and how, even when garments are layered, they still have the same outline.

This sketchbook shows interesting examples of silhouettes collected from magazines.

inspirational silhouettes w details certain structures or use of fabric.

over-sized

GILES

GIVENC

layers creating volume on only one side

interesting effect a sleeve

**WORKOUT
30**

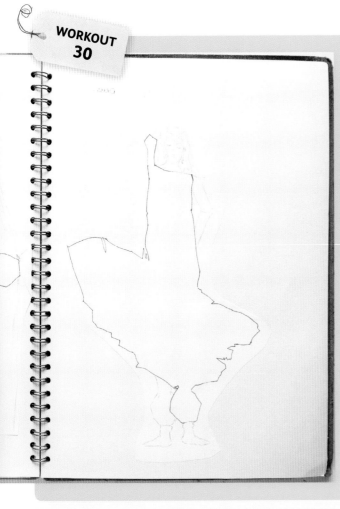

Make your own silhouettes

Generate your own silhouettes with the help of a friend
or using a dress stand. Take approximately 5 m (15 ft) of
plain fabric and wrap around the figure, by tucking, tying,
or folding it. Use line drawings to record the results. You
could also try cutting out simple shapes from coloured
paper or felt and placing these onto the
outline of a figure.

TWO APPROACHES
The line drawing on the left
shows a silhouette created by
wrapping fabric around a figure.
The silhouette on the right was
created with simple cut-out
shapes. Use these approaches
to make outlines that are not
obviously practical but that can
be referred to for inspiration.

Change ready-made silhouettes

Mix and match your own clothes to make different
silhouettes and photograph the results. Combine separates,
for example, blouses and trousers or jackets and skirts, for
more interesting results.

*A black-and-white
printed scarf nips in
the waist of this
directional combination
of clashing prints.*

USE CLASSIC SHAPES
Here the designer has
explored the classic
1950s hourglass
silhouette. Belts have
been used to draw
attention to the waist.
Using tight-fitting
clothes over loose
garments can create
unusual shapes.

*A voluminous padded jacket
layered with a tight-fitting
football top, with a simple
leather belt at the waist,
creates a new outline.*

*A studded leather
belt cinches in a
blouson top and
crochet skirt.*

**WORKOUT
31**

Building a colour palette

As a designer you need to get used to identifying and choosing the colours that you want to use in your collection. All of the colours in a collection should work together so the customer can "mix and match". Also, imagine going into a store where your collection sits with several other designers on the sales floor – the more focused and cohesive your palette, the better your work will stand out.

You can work with colours that you like, or you can try to predict trends for each season. Professional trend forecasters are used in fashion, and many other industries, to propose trends up to four years ahead, which means that predicting this or next season's colour can be difficult. If you want to make a statement, choosing your own palette is the way to go.

MAKING COLOUR CHOICES
There are thousands of colours, and each one can be a fashion statement. Honing your sense of colour is vital.

WORKOUT
32

Mix your own colours

To improve your understanding of colour, find patterns or images you are attracted to and try matching the colours by mixing them with paint, such as gouache. Make a note of how you arrived at the correct colour. You could also try finding a marker pen to match to each colour. Alternatively, collect appropriate matching yarns and fix them to the page, wrapped into small, circular bundles.

Pantone
367

Pantone
159

Pantone
7489

Pantone
1815

Make a note of names or code numbers of colours you have matched. If mixing paint colours, record the proportions of colours used.

KEEP SAMPLES THAT CATCH YOUR EYE
Matching colours is a great way of exploring colour. Make coloured swatches using pens, pencils, or paints, or wrap short lengths of yarn around fingers of card.

Choose colours

Select an image that you like and choose colours from it. Divide them into key or core colours, which are the background colours that dominate the image, and accent or highlight colours, which are the bright or contrasting colours that appear less frequently.

Alternatively, you can generate your own imagery by taking photographs of manmade or natural scenes. Remember that foliage changes colour throughout the year, and that the light changes continually, giving subtle changes to each photograph you take. You can keep a file of these photos for future reference.

IDENTIFY THE CONTRASTS
The colours of the illuminated building (above) have been divided into core colours of blacks and browns with highlights of bright yellow. The natural world can often throw up unusual and dramatic juxtapositions of colour (left). Here the key colours are dark greys and browns taken from the rocky outcrops. The accent colours are the fiery yellow and orange provided by the river of lava flowing across the scene.

Make sure you keep a record of the exact shades you have chosen by labelling them clearly with their name, number, or how you mixed them.

BE ALERT TO COLOUR
Always be on the lookout for pleasing or surprising colour combinations to add to your collection. Once you start looking, you will find them all around you. Try to explore both bright artificial colours and subtle natural tones. Although you may initially be drawn to one colour palette, your research may offer new possibilities.

Mood/ inspirations:

MOOD/ COLOUR WAYS: Black
Gold
Candy red
Mint green
Deep purple

INSPIRATIONS: "Charlie and the chocolate factory" is the origin of my research. I will take various elements from the film and translate them into ideas for print and silhouette.

Using knit

The process of producing and using knit is exciting and rewarding. Knit is a huge industry and is used in the majority of menswear and womenswear collections. Some labels, such as Tse, Malo, and Missoni, are built on knitwear. It is comfortable and versatile. It also adds a textural element to a range or collection and contrasts well with woven fabrics.

See also
APPLYING TEXTURE,
PAGES 50–51

Research knitwear

Look at where knit is used in an existing collection. Has the designer used fully fashioned knits or "cut and sew" knits, such as T-shirts? Have they used patterns and graphics? Make notes in your sketchbook.

Start to think about how you might design knitwear. You can ask most yarn suppliers for small samples of yarn to make up your own cards. As with woven fabrics, try to go for as wide a range of ply, weights, twists, colours, and compositions as possible.

WORKOUT 34

MARGOT
35% Mohair - 90% Lana
35% Zurn
Nm 700

MERLINO G
35% Mohair - 50% Seta

MURANO G
60% Mohair - 5% Volpa
35% Lana
Nm 1800

10% Lana

CINIGLIA SETA
100% Seta

WORKOUT 36

Reclaim yarns

WORKOUT 35

New, good-quality yarns can be quite expensive. Look through old knitwear. If you like a particular colour, thickness, or composition of yarn and want a sample of it, simply unravel the garment.

DON'T GET IN A KNOT
Wind the yarn carefully into a ball or onto a card to prevent knots. Try to jot down the composition of the yarn from the garment label.

Make your own knitwear

Knit gives you lots of exciting opportunities to use texture (see workout 37) and colour and pattern. Traditionally, pattern is worked into the knit using intarsia and fair-isle techniques. Today you can buy computer programs that convert your graphics into knitting patterns. However, you will need access to the appropriate equipment and a good understanding of knitwear techniques before you start experimenting.

Machine knitting is fast, but takes time to master. Hand-knitting can be a slow process, but is easy to pick up – there are plenty of tutorials available online or in books, or ask friends and family if they can teach you. Try knitting a swatch of fabric in an interesting yarn you have collected.

USE KNITTING MACHINES
Many schools and colleges have knitting machines and will give you a tutorial before you get started.

Use texture

Knitwear works particularly well in creating texture. For this task you will need thin cartridge paper and some crayons.

Make rubbings of different surfaces such as bark, wood grain, stone, concrete, shells and other natural forms. Using yarns appropriate to the task, knit these textures into samples that suggest the same pattern and weight as the surfaces that inspired them. There are plenty of stitch collection books available in book stores.

When knitting it is important to keep a record of the type of stitches you have used and how many are in each row. With this information you can use a variety of yarns that do not correspond to your original rubbing. Try using slinky or very fine yarns or soft, mohair-type yarns, tapes and ribbons. This should result in new and interesting knit textures.

REFER TO NATURE
Above and left, a knitwear range that was inspired by sea creatures.

UNDER THE SEA
The Nudibranch sea slug (below) inspired this knitwear piece on the right.

Using print

Print is pattern applied with dyes that sits on the surface of a fabric. It can be incredibly diverse, from pretty florals to angular geometrics, to watercolour effects; from pretty and feminine to the avant-garde. Print also serves to bring a colour story together, unifying solid-colour separates so they read as one collection. As with knit, some designers specialize in producing designs with printed fabrics.

See also
BUILDING A COLOUR PALETTE,
PAGES 30–31
USING CAD,
PAGES 52–53

Research print design

WORKOUT
38

Anything can inspire your print work, from photographs or drawings, to artworks and sculpture. Look for elements in a visual that could be used as separate motifs or work well when repeated. Examples include a composition, use of colour, and "directional" images that will continue to look contemporary and fresh.

Select a series of images that fall into one or more of the above categories; some prints can be tonal, others graphic. Photocopy or scan them, cut them out, and stick them onto drawings or photographs of fashion figures. Use them at different scales and repeat some of the motifs in geometric or linear patterns. You could use several different print ideas in different scales and colourways on one figure, or you may not want to cover the whole figure in print.

In this collection, print has been confined to the upper body.

Try basic prints

WORKOUT
39

Print can be produced quickly, but often comprises many technically demanding processes. To make a really easy print, and have some fun, try making potato prints. Carve out a simple image, or number of images, such as stars, circles, or other geometric shapes. Ink the potato's surface with a print medium and experiment with different shapes in your sketchbook.

■ **Don't forget** to try varying the colour of the fabric background, or putting coloured washes down first.

CHOOSE YOUR BLOCKS
These examples on the left show traditional carved Indian wood blocks. Making wood blocks can be a time-consuming and difficult process. Linoleum is much easier to carve into. Both are available from craft shops. Easier still are potato prints, such as those below.

WORKOUT
40

Play with prints

Look at existing prints that you like. A great way to practise designing print is to scan original fabrics or wallpapers and use a computer program, such as Photoshop, to resize and recolour them. Make sure you make the print your own by mixing imagery from several different sources, and record the results in your sketchbook.

KEEP IT SIMPLE
Prints, such as the one on the far left, can be complex, with lots of depth, or simple and highly graphic. The print on the left has been adapted from the more complicated original, and focuses on a simple spot-and-line composition.

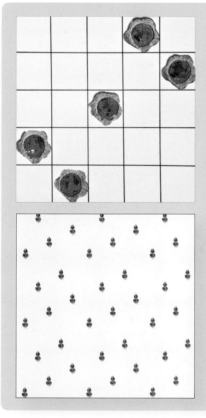

WORKOUT
41

Make a five-spot repeat

Select a print motif that is no larger than 4 x 4 cm (2 x 2 in.). When you first do this task it is easier to use a series of photocopied images all the same size that you stick into place. Using a ruler, draw a 25 cm (10 in.) square. Divide this into 4 cm (2 in.) sections to make a grid.

Place one print motif in the centre of one square in each row, in separate columns – you should not have more than one motif in each row or column. You can rotate more complex motifs, at 90 or 180 degrees for example, to add to the design interest of your print. Once you have created your five-spot pattern, known as a printing block, photocopy it several times. Stick the grids next to each other to form your five-spot repeat.

Try the task again, this time experimenting with different motifs.

SPOT THE REPEAT
The image above shows a basic five-spot repeat pattern. The image below shows a five-spot repeat that has been extended to cover a length of fabric. Can you work out the original arrangement of the five spots on the grid?

Making your sketchbook work

You have already completed your initial research and will have started sampling and drawing. Your research is probably quite general, for example, finding out about historical fashion, looking at what people wear, and how to draw them. Now is a good time to add to the primary research in your sketchbook. You will use this new imagery as the starting point for your collection. The collection will incorporate many of the ideas from your sketchbook and help make sense of the ideas and imagery that you have already collected and started to interpret.

WORKOUT 42

Choose a theme

A good way to begin organizing your thoughts is by identifying a theme from your existing work. The best themes are usually nothing to do with fashion. As you have been exploring exhibitions and museums and reading a range of literature, hopefully a theme will spring to mind. You can also work from ideas that have inspired you throughout your life. These themes can be quite literal, such as working with nature, examples of which might be butterflies, flowers, and sea shells. Alternatively, you may want to choose more abstract ideas derived from your life, such as childhood, identity, and relationships. You could work directly from historical visual sources, such as paintings or eras and movements in art.

SHOW AN INFLUENCE
The Gaultier collection below shows a strong pirate influence. You might find your influences leave a more subtle footprint on your final collection.

DEVELOP A THEME
This image from the early days of film (right) could be developed into a theme based on the 1920s.

JEAN PAUL GAULTIER

Other possible themes
- Ancient Egypt
- Androgeny
- Architecture
- Childhood memories
- Circus
- Classical Greek and Roman statues
- Cowboys
- Distorting the body
- Fairies
- Film icons or films
- Gothic
- National or historical costume
- Nature
- Origami
- Oversized/undersized
- Paintings and artists
- Personal feelings
- Punk and other music influences
- Science fiction
- The weather
- Traditional and historical costume
- Vintage sportswear

WORKOUT 43

Research the theme

Visit the library to find additional imagery and take photocopies of anything relevant to your theme. You can also look on the Internet for related information. It is often better if the imagery you start with is not deliberately fashion based. Try to look at your theme from as many different angles as possible. For example, if you are researching an era, try to find out about the news, celebrities, how people lived, and fashions. You will eventually find some elements that catch your eye – you can organize these into a mood board (see workout 7).

ENLARGE YOUR THEME
This mood board (above) focuses on black-and-white photography of celebrities of the 1920s.

WHAT INTERESTS YOU?
This geisha is wearing a kimono that could form part of a theme on traditional Japanese life.

WORKOUT 44

Relate fabrics to the theme

Start to think about fabrics in relation to your overall idea. You have probably already collected lots of fabric samples. Look through them and see which ones relate to your theme, or could. Collect other fabrics you would like to work with and stick or staple these into your sketchbook. Use several weights of fabric, some knit, and maybe a novelty fabric to create a well-balanced fabric story.

BRING IT TOGETHER
How do the fabrics you are interested in work together? Do the textures complement or contrast with each other? Think back to your work on colour and look at your theme in terms of base and accent fabrics.

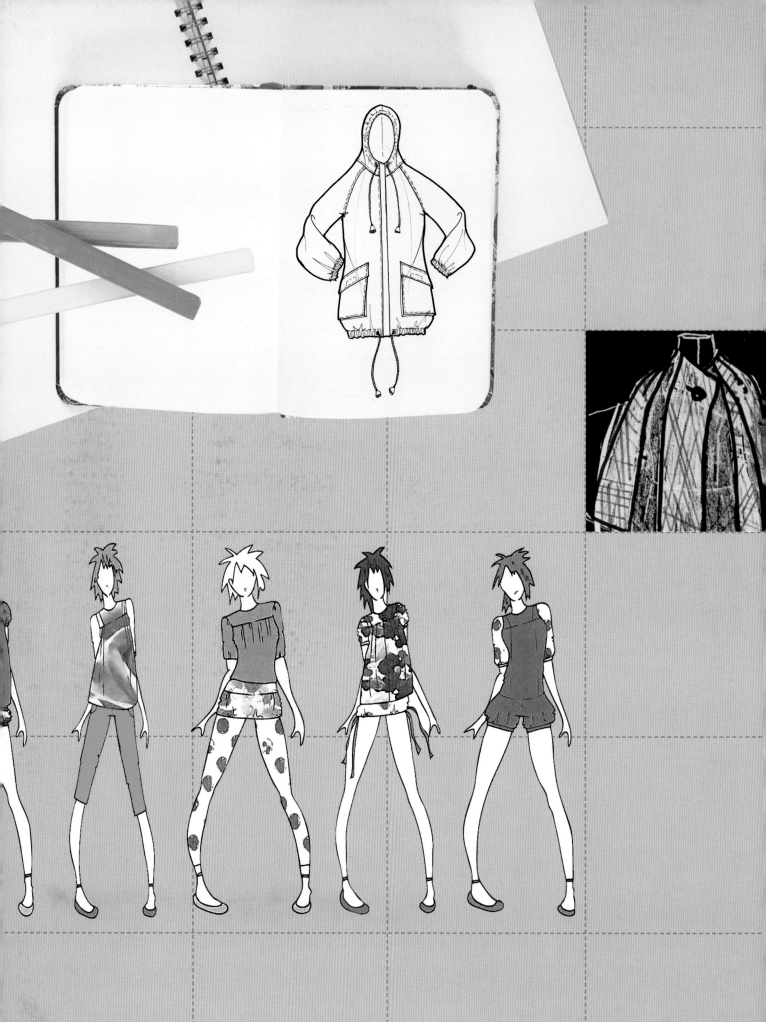

Chapter two:

Drawing & designing

Drawing the figure and garments accurately is essential for a successful designer, and these workouts focus on these skills, building up to creating your look and putting together your first collection line-ups.

The figure and proportion

Drawing the figure that you are going to base your designs on is a crucial first step towards developing your own visual language for fashion design. If you correctly capture the shape and proportion of the figure on paper, you will soon be able to produce designs that will ultimately be turned into garments. Getting the figure right for your needs means that it is easier to get the proportions of the garments right – and, as Alexander McQueen would say, fashion is all about proportion.

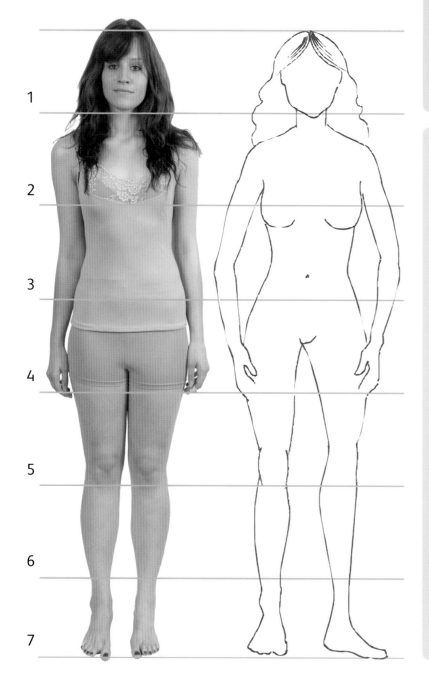

See also
DRAWING EXPRESSIVE FIGURES,
PAGE 44

WORKOUT 45

Study the figure

Traditionally, the human figure divides vertically into seven heads. To test this for yourself, pick out photographs of people in magazines and see how many "heads" fit into the figure. Measure out a variety of figures, both men and women, to see how people vary – quite often the results are very different from this general rule.

WORKOUT 46

Be accurate

It is important that you can accurately depict the male or female form before you begin work on your exaggerated fashion figure (see workout 53). Remember that men tend to have wider shoulders and broader necks than women, while women generally have narrower waists and wider hips, and, of course, a bust.

Practice drawing male and female figures, using the photographs you have collected for guidance if necessary. Get the figure in proportion by measuring a person using your thumb and pencil. Hold your pencil at arm's length in front of you and align the top of the pencil with the top of the subject's head. Use your thumb to define the bottom of the head. This will be "one-head measurement". Keeping your arm straight, work down the figure to see how many "one-head measurements" fit into the full figure.

Draw from life

Developing a full knowledge of the proportions of the body can also be achieved through life drawing. You can enrol in classes or draw your friends and family.

A good way to practise is to make quick figure drawings every day, even if only for ten minutes. Work on each pose for one or two minutes at the most, using a medium such as charcoal or markers, which enable large drawings to be done quickly and without getting caught up in the fine detail.

MAKE PENCIL YOUR FIRST CHOICE
Pencil drawings (left) are the easiest to achieve, as you should always be carrying a pencil. They are quick and convenient and provide the opportunity for fine work to indicate detailing and shading.

ADD TONE AND VOLUME
"Cross-hatching" (building up an area with criss-crossing lines) is a good way to add tonal values and give 3D volume to the body (see left). The colour has been indicated on top of the pen with coloured pencils and markers in a very quick, loose manner.

CAPTURE IMAGES FAST
These drawings (above) were made from a TV programme and show that you can achieve very life-like drawings without necessarily using "real" subjects – but they need to be captured quickly. Watercolour and pen, used here, are ideal media for speedily indicating colour, volume, and different layers of fabrics.

Drawing the face

The face is the focus of your drawing. It is the point that the viewer's eyes are drawn to, and it anchors the rest of the figure to the page. Capturing the "right" face is also an excellent way of developing the look of your figure, and you can play with hair and make-up designs to complement the rest of the outfit.

Get to know the basic face

Before you can begin to experiment with face drawing, you need to familiarize yourself with the basic face.

Draw an egg shape and divide it into two vertically, then into quarters horizontally. The top of the eyes will sit on the halfway line, the hairline should be around the top quarter mark, and the bottom of the nose will end at the bottom of the third quarter. The centre of the mouth will be halfway down in the bottom quarter.

LINE THEM UP
Of course there are slight variations between people. You can try drawing these lines on photographs of faces to see how often the rule applies, and see how it varies.

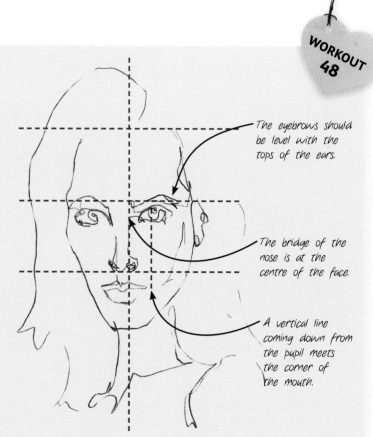

The eyebrows should be level with the tops of the ears.

The bridge of the nose is at the centre of the face.

A vertical line coming down from the pupil meets the corner of the mouth.

WORKOUT 48

Add make-up

Come up with some make-up looks for different situations – for example, to go to school or work in, for meeting friends, or for going out to dinner or an exciting nightclub. Think about different fashion looks, such as boho, goth, indie, and other more experimental youth movements. You can also get inspiration from your historical research.

GO WILD
Have fun experimenting with make-up designs. Here, a romantic look based on Sixties false eyelashes has been accessorized with absinthe green nail polish.

WORKOUT 49

Add hair

Keep a "hair library" at the back of your sketchbook – go through magazines and tear out interesting hair shapes, styles, and colours that you find, so when you design a collection, you can select a hairstyle that will best compliment your mood and inspiration.

Try to create or adapt ten new, or interesting, hairstyles, using your hair library as a starting point. You can be very creative with the look you propose for your model. Experiment with different media for different types of hairstyles. Marker pens work well for bobbed hair, sharp, coloured pencils for longer, straighter hair, and water-based paint for curly hair. Allow, too, for the medium you are most comfortable with.

GO BACK IN TIME
You may want to refer to some of your historical research for inspirational starting points for your hair designs.

Hairstyle based around a 1950s Teddy boy haircut adapted for a woman.

1960s straight haircut with Alice band. Accessories and clips can be used to enhance and add to your hairstyle.

1970s perm.

A classic "Rachel" cut inspired by the TV show Friends in the late 1990s.

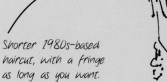

Shorter 1980s-based haircut, with a fringe as long as you want.

Drawing expressive figures

Being able to draw is an asset if you want to work in fashion. Drawings that bring a certain expressiveness and lifelike quality to the figure are preferable to other styles of drawing. The more lifelike or "fluid" you can make the figure, the more convincing the rendition of the garments will be. Your design will appear better proportioned and the garments more wearable and therefore desirable.

See also
STUDY THE FIGURE,
PAGE 40

DRAWING IN DIFFERENT MEDIA,
PAGE 48

WORKOUT 51

Do a warm-up

Before drawing a figure, try this warm-up. Use as many different media as you can and vary the width and darkness of a line by drawing lightly and with force, without taking your drawing tool off the paper.

MAKE YOUR MARK
Charcoal is a wonderful medium to start with. It's soft and smudgy and not at all easy to control, and it's this quality that allows you to be so expressive.

WORKOUT 52

Draw people in action

Your life-drawing skills should be progressing well. If you haven't already, it can be fun to enrol in a class with a proper model and an instructor who will set you new challenges as you improve. One way to take your life drawing further is to try to draw people when they are moving. It is great if you can get into a rehearsal session for dancers, or study athletes at a training session. Look at the photographs of Muybridge, Futurist works of art, and *Nude Descending a Staircase* by Marcel Duchamp. If you aren't already familiar with these then look them up on the Internet and see what you can find out.

WORKOUT 53

Exaggerate the figure

Once you are confident drawing the real human body, you can develop a more exaggerated, fashion-based figure. This is generally "eight-heads" tall (see workout 46) with a high waist and long legs for a women, shorter legs for a man. In the standard fashion "high-hip pose," the shoulder and hip angles are opposite.

LOOK AT THE LINES
Look in a mirror, hands on hips with one leg bearing all your weight, and see which hip is higher and which shoulder is lower.

Exaggerate the line across the shoulders and through the waist and hips to create more dynamic movement in the figure. This will make the model look less static, and give the clothes better drape.

The support leg is always right under the clavicle bone (the pit of the neck) to balance the figure. This helps create an "S curve" that gives your figure movement and attitude.

EMPHASIZE THE LINE
These line sketches show an exaggerated silhouette in development, and right, the figure in its finished marker-drawn form. Look at the Web site of the Powerhouse Museum in Sydney, Australia (www.powerhousemuseum.com) where you will find some wonderful vintage fashion illustrations.

When to use a medium

Designers make choices based on personal preference, but these are underpinned by a sound understanding of what they are trying to achieve. This is especially true when selecting and working with drawing media.

When it comes to drawing out your ideas and illustrating your collection – which are two entirely different processes – you need to feel confident with your medium, and to do this it has to be appropriate to the situation.

WORKOUT 54

Take visual notes

Most of the drawings that fashion designers make are line drawings, and they are quite often quick ones. For these you will need to use a medium such as a pen or a retractable pencil so that the lead doesn't keep breaking.

Start with pencil, and get comfortable with it; you can erase and perfect the drawing. You can advance to pen later. Pencil will also help you to learn how line quality – its density or thickness – can communicate depth and shadow, or fabric weight. Make some quick sketches in your visual diary.

WORKOUT 55

Do quick designs

Design drawings are usually made with black and coloured pens. Try making some quick designs that you think are sympathetic to your figure, using something similar to a black fibre-tip pen. Now add colour – the easiest way is with marker pens. Make sketches on a full figure, but also make "detail shots" of top stitching, for example.

■ **Don't forget** that professionals use Pantone pens, which have an international colour standard so that your production department knows the exact shade you require.

DRAW THE DETAILS
These drawings depict a complex design range. Work like this is very useful when you have a complete look to draw up and can give you information on all the details. The use of a fairly fine pen will allow you to see all the relevant details.

Finding your style

Illustration is more akin to artwork and as such allows for much more artistic freedom. Your style will evolve, so the type of illustrations you do now will change in the future, but you can start to shape personal illustrative style by experimenting with illustrating either some of your own early designs, or designs you find in magazines. The medium, or media, you choose for your illustrations can reflect the spirit of the designs.

MAKE VISUAL RECORDS
Your illustrations are an indication of the "feel" of the collection, rather than more factual design work or photographs. They are used to provide a record of what you have made, to provide information on further outfits you want to make, and to build a portfolio.

These quick illustrations have been done in pen outline with marker over the top. There is quite a lot of white paper showing through, suggesting the collection is light and free.

In this highly feminine and youthful illustration, note the depiction of sheer fabric on the upper part of the bodice and on the embellishment for the bust, as well as the bows on the shoes, which enhance the look. The illustration has been drawn then scanned into Photoshop.

This fairly quick drawing, filled with watercolour, gives the overall impression of an ideas-based look.

Drawing in different media

This section is all about putting pen to paper in the correct manner. Some media, such as pens and pencils, are self-explanatory, and how you use them is obvious. However, there are other media used by fashion designers that you may not be familiar with – but soon will be with a little practice.

See also
DRAWING EXPRESSIVE FIGURES,
PAGE 44

WORKOUT 57

Use a photocopier or scanner

The photocopier is a useful tool that is easy to work, although it can be expensive. It is excellent for changing collection line-ups (see workout 86), resizing artwork for rough designs, working out basic prints, and particularly for photocopying fabric to use in collage.

Take some photocopies or scan some images of models from magazines. These will be your "base" figures. You will need to print these out. Then use photocopied imagery of garments, motifs, and pieces of textiles to collage on top of the image. When you are satisfied with the results, scan or photocopy the image again.

EXPERIMENT WITH IDEAS
For this knitwear collection using collage on a "base" figure, animal motifs have been used in differing scales to show appliqué ideas. The designer has added a "painterly" background to counteract the more graphic feel of the work.

Use gouache

Gouache is opaque watercolour and can be used alone or combined with other media. Gouache paints give vibrant results. They produce a richly coloured rendering with an attractive, velvety finish to the painted surface.

Choose a basic design for an outfit or accessory and apply colour using gouache paint.

WORKOUT 58

WORK IN LAYERS
Unlike watercolour, gouache is opaque and can be used, as here, to layer light tones over dark to create graphic form and pattern.

Use pencils

Pencils can be used either alone or in combination with other media; they are versatile and great for details. Contour outlines on the figure and clothing are easy to draw with pencils. Sketchbooks are a perfect place to use them.

This medium is perfect for a layered approach – try using a base layer of markers or watercolours on a design followed by pencils for surface texture.

WORKOUT 59

ADD SHADING AND TONE
Pencils come in a wide variety of colours but here a tonal approach and careful shading have been used to show form.

Use watercolours

Watercolours and watercolour pencils are excellent when an illustration calls for a blended application. Watercolour pencils combine the luminous colour of watercolours with the ease of use and portability of pencils.

Try using watercolour pencils as you would normal pencils to shade in your design, then blend them with a wet brush.

WORKOUT 60

BLEND TONES
Watercolours and watercolour pencils create a smooth finish. A deft touch is needed to avoid muddy colour effects, streaking, and over-blended areas.

Use pastels

Pastels enable you to get a full colour and value effect and create a feeling for form by using light and shadow. Buy a set that contains at least two values of each colour – a light and dark – to enable you to draw form, or you could start with just white, grey, and black to try out the medium.

Apply colour to an outfit or accessory design with pastels, emphasizing form with light and dark shades. Experiment with smudging them together.

WORKOUT 61

SMUDGE SHADES
Pastels are so soft they can be blended by smudging them together, but take care not to smudge them accidentally. You can fix your finished drawing with a spray fixative.

Applying texture

Depicting the correct fabrics is an important aspect of fashion drawing. You can do this through photocopying, or scanning and printing original fabrics, or CAD techniques (see pages 52–53). However, most good illustrations use some traditional drawing.

WORKOUT 62

Depict thick fabrics

Pick a thick fabric, such as a tweed, and try to illustrate it. It can be useful to think of thicker fabrics as layers. For example, lay down a base of gouache, leave it to dry, and work over it in pastel or coloured pencil, aiming to build up layers of colour to replicate the textured layers of the fabric you are representing.

■ **Don't forget** that the same technique can also be tried with knitted textures.

Here a marker layer with crayon laid over the top achieves the check effect.

Coloured pencil has been used here for a subtle look.

Fine marker pen gives a bolder tone.

An under-layer of gouache has had a pencil check worked over the top.

GET THE EFFECT
Different approaches have been used to show pattern and texture on these coats. The two illustrations on the left have been made with one type of media, the two above have used mixed media. Which approach works better?

Illustrate sheer fabrics

Now try drawing sheer fabrics, such as those used to make tights, which are some of the hardest textures to replicate. Lay down a flesh tone in marker pen to indicate the body beneath the fabric, then work over this in very sharp pencil, using curved cross-hatching strokes.

■ **Don't forget** that you could also use washes of acrylic or watercolour paint.

1 Draw the outline of the legs lightly in pencil.

2 Lay down a bare colour to indicate the flesh; here marker pen has been used.

3 When dry, begin working in the colour of the stockings with cross-hatching.

4 Continue until the drawing is complete. Varying the tone in parts gives a sense of form.

Draw textured fabrics

Drawing strongly textured fabric takes some time. To get the scale, relate the scale of the grid to your eyes, then relate it to your figure's eyes, or the hand is another good measuring device. A key to conveying texture is the contour "holding line" around the garment. Is it fuzzy, smooth, or angular? How can the contour line express texture?

Choose some textural fabrics that are quite repetitious in their design and construction and try to draw them using a pencil. You can show them on appropriate garment shapes you have designed yourself or work from real garments.

■ **Don't forget** it's not worth trying for an exact replication of the fabrics, as this is virtually impossible. Try to give an impression of what is in front of you.

You can be quite sketchy with this type of work and can leave in your guidelines so that you can apply the pattern accurately.

The fuzzy contour line helps define the woolly texture.

GET IT RIGHT
These drawings indicate different types of fabric by just using pencil. On the left is a herringbone women's jacket, and on the right an Aran knit men's cardigan with cables and ribs.

Using CAD

Understanding CAD (computer-aided design) is an essential requirement when working in the modern fashion industry, especially when dealing with the more technical side of drawing, such as the production of working drawings and collection line-ups (see pages 74–75). These basic exercises will get you started.

The programs used here are Photoshop and Illustrator, part of Adobe CS3 for Apple Macintosh. When you are comfortable with it, this software will allow you a large degree of flexibility as a drawing tool.

WORKOUT 65

Change colours in a print

Scan in a pattern and try using Photoshop to change the constituent colours. Think about tone and colour, and change individual elements.

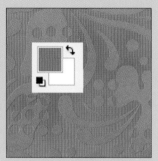

1 Open your scanned image of a pattern. Choose the Paint Bucket tool from the toolbox. In Tool Options, make sure the "contiguous" box is not checked.

2 Choose your new colour by clicking on the Foreground Color box in the toolbox and selecting the shade you want.

3 Use the Paint Bucket tool to click on the colour you want to replace, and it will be flooded with the new colour, here white.

4 Repeat with other colours you wish to replace. Here the original green has been replaced with black.

WORKOUT 66

Add pattern to a skirt

Scan in a line drawing of a skirt or create your own using the techniques described opposite. You can then add pattern in Photoshop.

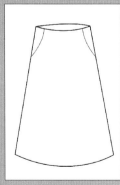

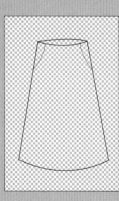

1 Open a line drawing of a skirt. Select black lines only (Select>Color range>Select: shadows).

2 Copy the selected lines. Create a new layer (Layer>New) and paste the lines onto it.

3 Select the area outside of the skirt using the Magic Wand tool and copy and paste it onto a new layer.

4 Paste your chosen print design onto a new layer and Send to Back (Layer>Arrange).

5 Your skirt outline will appear filled with your print design.

Draw a T-shirt

Follow these instructions to create the outline of a basic T-shirt in Illustrator. The body of the T-shirt is drawn separately from the sleeves so that you can visualize the proportions of each section of the garment independently and check whether they are correct.

To begin any new piece of work in Illustrator, open a new Print Document, reset the workspace (Window>Work>Basic), and make sure you can see your rulers (View>Show Rulers).

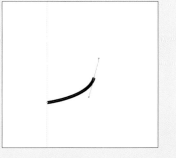

1 Click and drag a guideline from the vertical ruler to the centre of your Artboard. Select the Pen tool and, near the top of your guideline, click once to set down an anchor point. At the next anchor point, click and hold down the mouse button, then drag up to pull out a pair of Curve Handles.

2 Use the Curve Handles to adjust the curve so it forms half of the neckline. Once you are happy with the curve, let go of the mouse button. Put your Pen back on the last anchor point and click once to set the curve. The leading Curve Handle will disappear.

3 You can now place your next anchor point to form the shoulder of the T-shirt. Continue forming the outline of the T-shirt body. After a little practice, you will find this as easy as using a pen or pencil.

4 Continue until you have half the outline of a sleeveless T-shirt. Using the Selection tool (black arrow), click on the outline of your T-shirt. A blue Bounding Box will appear around your drawing.

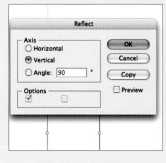

5 Go to Object>Transform>Reflect to open the reflect dialogue box. Choose a Vertical axis and click Copy. Click on the reflected copy and hold down the shift key on the keyboard to keep it aligned as you drag it into position.

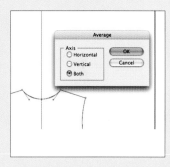

6 Choose the Direct Selection tool (white arrow). Starting from outside the T-shirt, drag a selection box over the two anchor points in the centre of the collar. Go to Object>Path>Average, choose Both and click OK.

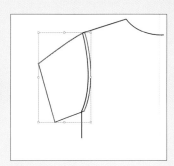

7 Choose the Pen tool again and draw a sleeve. Follow the line of the sleeve hole but overlap it slightly. Using the Selection tool, select the sleeve and go to Object>Arrange>Send to Back. Reflect, copy, and position the other sleeve.

8 Draw the back of the neckline as shown and join it up around the front so that it forms a continuous shape.

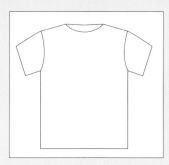

9 Select the neckline and choose Send to Back as before. Your T-shirt is complete.

Developing the theme

You can now begin to transfer the imagery and ideas from the research you did earlier into garment shapes and decorative ideas. Designers tend to fall into two main categories, structuralists and decorators, but at this stage in your fashion career you should aim to keep a foot in both camps.

See also

EXPLORING SILHOUETTE

PAGES 28–29

USING PRINT

PAGES 34–35

WORKOUT
68

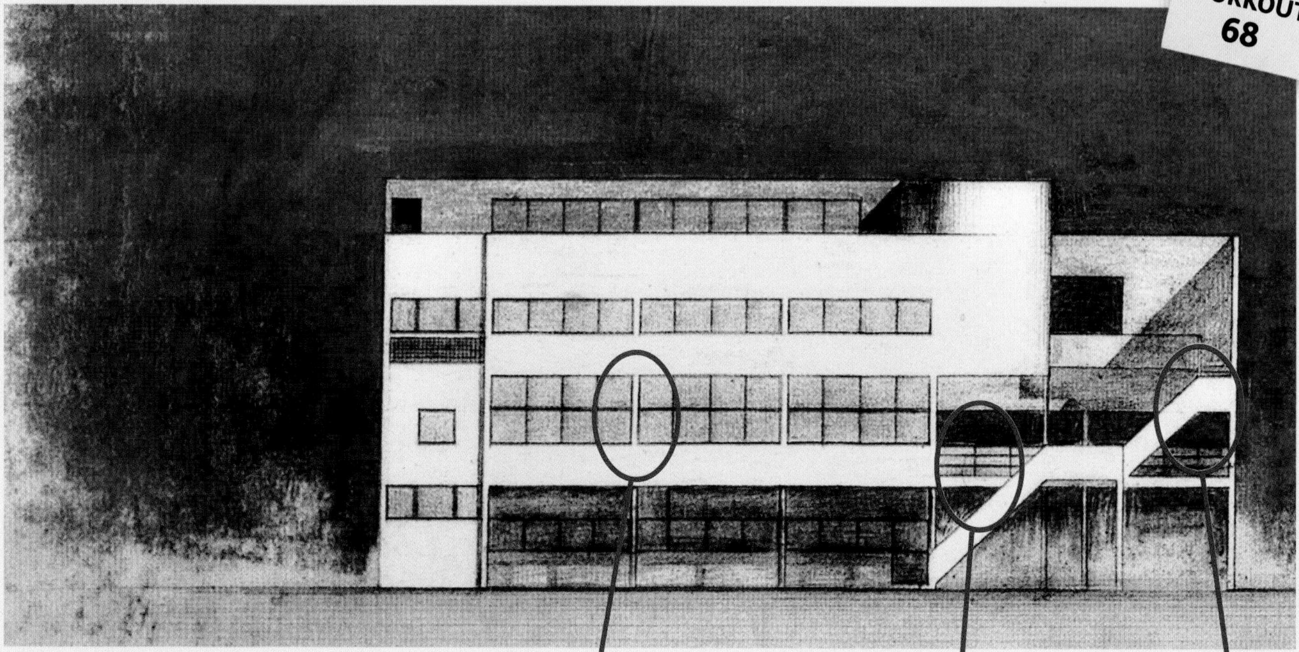

Take inspiration from the structuralists

Structuralists specialize in innovative shapes or tailoring. Choose an existing garment by a contemporary or historical designer famous for their structured clothes and try to find out what inspired them. Look at the complete silhouette, or just areas of a garment, such as the sleeve shape or the front fastening.

CONSTRUCT A DESIGN
This menswear collection (right) shows details and structure taken directly from these Bauhaus buildings (above). The inserts in the trousers and shirts are based on the shapes of windows, the angles come from the stairway, and the whole look is meant to appear as if it has been pieced together with building construction techniques.

WORKOUT
69

Take inspiration from decorators

Decorators focus on pattern and embellishment. Try and find some designers famous for their use of colour or pattern and research their work.

Start to explore how you can make simply shaped clothes unique by using innovative decoration. Try using a basic A-line skirt silhouette and applying colour and pattern based on the colour palette and motifs available to you.

APPLY PATTERN
These Manish Arora dresses (far left) show a simple garment shape that has been heavily decorated with embroidery, appliqué, and prints based on the sights of Paris and London. Can you see where the Queen's Guard (left) have been used on the garments?

WORKOUT
70

Develop your own ideas

Take some of the imagery from your own research and start to manipulate it. Photocopy the imagery and place it on your figure. Try using it upside down, on its side, and at various sizes. See how it could be used throughout the collection in different garments. This is called "motif filtration" and is the cornerstone of a cohesive collection.

FIND A STARTING POINT
The work of artist Rachel Whiteread provided the inspiration for the cubed motif used in these early designs.

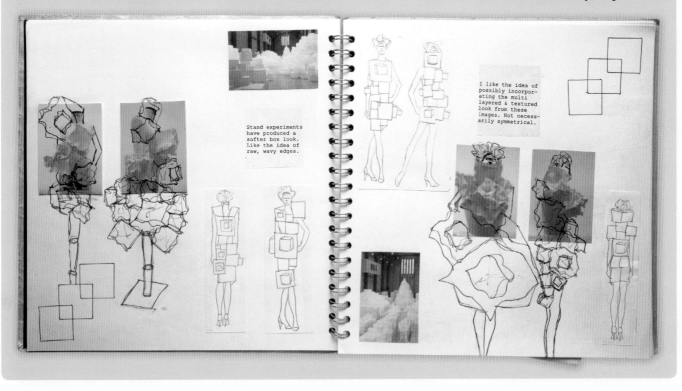

Stand experiments have produced a softer box look. Like the idea of raw, wavy edges.

I like the idea of possibly incorporating the multi layered & textured look from these images. Not necessarily symmetrical.

Applying your research

Now that you have all your ideas in place and have started your first tentative drawings, you can begin to develop your research into ideas for garments.

See also

FABRIC SAMPLING AND MANIPULATION

PAGES 58–59

WORKOUT 71

The design process

Look through your research and start to make links between your theme and fashion. Make drawings of your strongest ideas next to your images, identifying what interests you. This will give you a strong base for designing your first collection.

Here is an example of how research can be developed into a final garment. It starts with the chosen theme, a samurai costume, and shows how it progresses through sketchbooks and samples to the outfit opposite.

The first page of your sketchbook should quite clearly show where you are looking for inspiration. This samurai armour, seen at a museum exhibition, was the starting point for this project and eventually led to the garment shown on the opposite page.

SKIRTS DETAIL

PLEATED TROUSERS TIGHT AT CALF.

The next stage involves extensive research into your theme and note taking. These trousers have been drawn directly from a film still. You can see how they have been translated into the final garment opposite.

NOTE
MIX OF
PRIMARY +
SECONDARY
RESEARCH

The silhouette, with its
wide shoulders and
nipped-in waist, has been
drawn from the initial
theme and from research
into vintage Dior.

These pages link the wide shoulders of the
samurai costume to fashion, in this instance
historical Dior. There are also initial design
drawings: your sketchbook should be full of
rough ideas that can be developed later.

The initial research into samurai armour
produced some interesting ideas about pleats.
This photograph of a traditional Japanese
temple roof further feeds into the idea, and
has been translated into some fabric samples.

The pleated trousers, tight
at the calf, echo those
found during the initial
research into the theme of
samurai armour and bring in
the sample work on pleats.

Fabric sampling and manipulation

Sampling is the term that designers use when trying out ideas in fabric or other related materials on a small scale, before going into production. This process can be applied to new ideas, or to the translation of existing design details. Quite often the samples are produced in calico and can involve the use of tucks, pleats, and other methods of fabric manipulation.

See also
SEWING TECHNIQUES
PAGES 108–119

BOUND EDGE WITH GATHERING
You see bound edges everywhere, from the waistbands on skirts and trousers, to the collars and cuffs on jackets and shirts. They can vary in width from very fine finishes, seen in high-quality garments and fine fabrics, to very wide hems in thick wools on winter coats.

CROSS TUCKS
Make cross tucks by sewing lines of pin tucks (see right) in one direction and then rotating your fabric 90 degrees and sewing further lines of tucks to create a check effect.

Sew pin tucks

WORKOUT 72

Fold over your fabric and sew as close to the edge as you can. When you flatten the fabric again, you will be left with a pin tuck. Most often seen on the front of shirts or blouses and at the top of skirts, pin tucks can be used just about anywhere, in a decorative or functional manner. For an even effect, the distance between tucks must be measured, or they can be placed randomly, without measuring.

Try using pin tucks on an existing garment to gather in the fabric in certain areas. See how many you need to change the garment from loose-fitting to fitted.

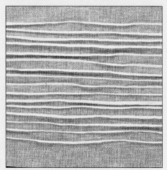

Making pin tucks is also an excellent general sewing exercise if you are unused to using a sewing machine.

Stitch pleats

WORKOUT 73

You can apply stitching to pleats in any design or direction or amount, as you see fit. Try it out on some differing pleating samples – some pencil-thin pleats, some much wider, some even pleats, some where the spacing is not controlled.

The pleats on the left have two lines of stitching across them to secure them.

BOX PLEATS
Most commonly seen on skirts and dresses, box pleats are constructed of a pair of equal, inverted folds. The top end of each pleat is sewn down in a square or rectangle – the "box" – with the bottom end left open.

RANDOM PLEATS
The pleats shown above are a mixture of box and simple knife pleats. Folds of different widths are sewn into place with a row, or rows, of stitching.

DARTS
Placed randomly as in this sample, darts can be used to create a decorative and three-dimensional effect.

QUILTING
Quilting involves sandwiching a layer of wadding between two layers of fabric, and holding the layers in place with rows of decorative stitching.

Try quilting

WORKOUT 74

To quilt accurately, you will need to measure where you want your rows of stitching to run. Use a ruler and iron-off crayon or pencil on top of the fabric.

Develop your own quilting patterns. You may want to apply these to different colours of fabric to see which are most visible. You may also want to vary the thickness of the wadding, again to see how visible you can make the quilted pattern.

Sew a channel seam with a contrast backing

WORKOUT 75

Sew two pieces of fabric together, as described for sewing a normal channel seam (right). However, sew them onto a backing fabric of a different colour, and when you unpick the central seam, do so only in parts. You can achieve the same look by sewing your first seam at measured intervals.

Experiment with using contrasting coloured fabrics, sewing or unpicking the gaps at different distances, and pressing or sewing the edges of the channel apart.

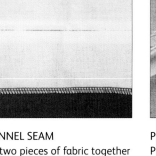

CHANNEL SEAM
Sew two pieces of fabric together using a large, loose stitch (tacking). Place another piece of fabric behind them, and sew two rows of stitching on either side of the seam, equal distances apart. Following this, unpick the central seam you sewed first, on the top layer of fabric. This leaves an open seam that is covered from behind.

PIPING
Piping is achieved in a similar way to a pin tuck (see workout 72) but cord is sewn into the tuck. If you use a zip foot on your sewing machine, you will be able to achieve very fine work and get very close to the edge of the piping. Piping can also be inserted into seams, and is most commonly seen as a trim on sportswear.

TRADITIONAL SHIRRING
Traditional shirring uses shirring elastic, which is sewn in lines to gather fabric, often to finish the edge of a garment. It is most suitable for mid-weight fabrics such as cotton lawns and jersey.

RANDOM SHIRRING
This technique involves gathering or puckering fabric using shirring elastic in a random pattern to create a decorative effect.

Add baby frills

WORKOUT 76

These decorative frills are strips of fabric gathered along a line of long, loose stitches and sewn onto a base fabric. Try attaching them onto the hem of a dress using different types and scales of printed fabrics.

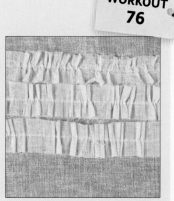

Sourcing fabrics and trims

As a fashion designer you need to be able to choose the right fabric for the task in hand. There are many, many different types of fabric, and knowledge of them will come with experience. This may take years, so don't worry if you can't name them all straight away.

Fabrics are organized into two main categories, natural and manmade (or synthetic). Natural fabrics include silk, cotton, linen, leather, latex, and wool from every source. Fabrics made from hemp, bamboo, and other natural sources are also available, although they are not common. Manmade fabrics include polyester, viscose, acrylic, acetate, nylon, and Lycra. There is also the weave of the fabric to consider, as in twill and herringbone.

See also
DRAPING,
PAGES 78–79

WORKOUT 77

Identify fabric composition

Pick out some old clothes and look at the care-labels to find out which fabrics they are made from. Look carefully at the weave and composition of each fabric type.

If the labels are too faded to read, or you have a fabric sample from an unknown source, try the burn test as a means of establishing the composition of the material. Cut a small square of fabric. Hold it in a pair of tweezers and carefully set it alight. Each fabric will have distinctive characteristics when burned (see panel, right). Make sure you carry out your burn tests in a well-ventilated area. Some manmade fabrics melt when burned, and the drips can burn your skin badly. You should take extra care when testing anything you suspect may be synthetic, and it is important to make sure there is a bowl of water underneath to put the fabric into.

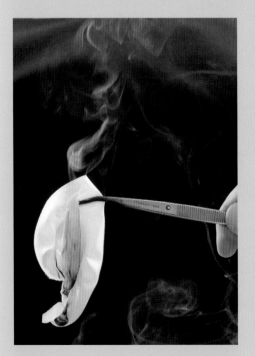

TRY A BURN TEST
The colour of the smoke, the smell, and the way the fabric burns will indicate what type of fabric you are testing.

What does it smell like?

- Cotton smells of burning paper and is very easy to blow out.

- Linen smells of burning leaves and is very easy to blow out.

- Silk smells of burning hair.

- Wool smells of burning hair and is difficult to keep alight.

- Polyester produces very black smoke and forms hard, rounded droplets when cool. Take extra care, because it will drip.

- Acetate smells of burning wood chips. Take extra care – like polyester, it will drip.

- Nylon smells strongly of burning plastic.

Make a fabric diary

Start a new sketchbook, small enough to carry around with you, exclusively for fabric samples. This is your fabric diary and it is a very important tool. Group similar fibres together so all the wools are in one area, the silks in another, and so on. Label them carefully and you will see that cottons, for example, come in many different weights and weaves or knits, and can serve many different purposes. Learn the names of weaves – not just "cotton" but "cotton poplin", "cotton voile", "cotton denim", "cotton twill".

■ **Don't forget** to collect a range of fabrics appropriate for different types of garments.

WORKOUT 78

The safest way of attaching the fabrics, so you don't lose them, is with a stapler.

This fabric diary includes information on where the fabric was found.

KEEP YOUR SAMPLES

These books show what your fabric diary may look like, with yarn and fabrics hanging out the sides and bottom – they may not look tidy but will be functional. The larger your fabric samples the better, and try and get each sample in more than one colour. Keep a note of each fabric's name (if it has one), the composition and weight, the width, and how much it costs.

Pages like this are useful for making comparisons between different types of similar fabrics.

Choosing Fabrics...

Applying details:
collars and necklines

How you apply collars and necklines influences the whole look of a top, and can make something special out of what would otherwise be a simple garment. Compare two jersey garments, a T-shirt and a polo shirt, and you will see that the shape is basically the same, but they look completely different due to the collar and neckline details.

WORKOUT 79

Experiment with necklines

Take a top that you have designed and erase the neckline, or redraw it without a neckline. Add in a new neckline, then see how many different necklines you can apply to your basic shape. You could include high and low necklines, such as roll or sweetheart necks, or turtlenecks or horseshoe necks.

When you are adding the details, think about the feel of the garment you are trying to create, and how each variation changes the design, to bring it more or less into line with original intentions.

A basic garment shape can be given a totally different feel with a change of neckline. Here, a high neck and long sleeves give a demure look.

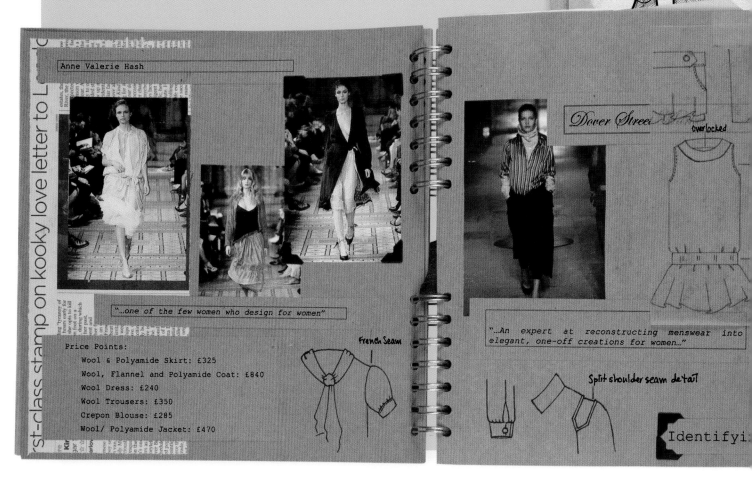

Anne Valerie Hash

"...one of the few women who design for women"

Price Points:
    Wool & Polyamide Skirt: £325
    Wool, Flannel and Polyamide Coat: £840
    Wool Dress: £240
    Wool Trousers: £350
    Crepon Blouse: £285
    Wool/ Polyamide Jacket: £470

French Seam

Dover Street

overlocked

"...An expert at reconstructing menswear into elegant, one-off creations for women..."

Split shoulder seam detail

Identifyi

A line of small buttons down the front enhances the mood of this dainty, lace-edged neckline.

LOOK AT NECKLINES

The sketches above show a basic A-line dress with a number of different necklines. From the top left moving clockwise, you have: a keyhole bound opening with a collar; a circular-cut frill neck with an additional large bow; a low, round neck with gathers at the centre front and embroidery detail; a sweetheart neck with gauging at the centre front bust and bands on the straps, followed by variations; then an envelope neck with a frill trim.

STUDY YOUR RESEARCH

Look through all the different variations on collars you have discovered from your research, as well as bows and ties of any shape or size.

Stitch detail

Market...

Applying details: **pockets**

Different types of garment require different types of pockets. Some of these pocket shapes are defined by tradition, such as on blazers, while others have a practical function, especially in sportswear. However, most are designed to enhance the look of a particular garment.

WORKOUT 80

Make a scrapbook

The easiest way to start designing pockets is to look at existing garments that have pockets as a feature, such as military jackets and trousers, performance sportswear, or even historical costume or vintage clothing, to get an idea of what can be achieved.

COLLECT POCKETS
Find a range of examples in different styles and from different eras and gather them together in a scrapbook. This collection of images has come from clothing catalogues and vintage magazines, old family photographs, and from books of copyright-free collections of fashion drawings, which are easily available from book stores.

Raid collections of old photographs and scan them; don't cut them up.

WORKOUT 81

Design pockets

From your research materials, sketch new pocket styles by mixing and matching, adding, or subtracting from the existing pockets.

SKETCH IDEAS
You will be amazed how many different designs you can come up with once you get started.

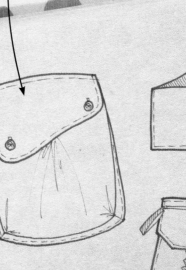

You can pick up bundles of old magazines from charity shops.

Examples of pocket designs on a range of garments, including this shirtwaist dress.

WORKOUT 82

Incorporate pockets into a garment

Try the pockets developed in the previous workout on garments. Use sketches to explore where to place the pockets, how large to have them, and how many to use.

This pocket detail would probably be too big for an actual garment.

Interesting asymmetric treatment.

Applying details: **fastenings**

Fastenings are the items that are used to close two pieces of fabric within a garment. They include buttons, buttonholes and loops; zips; ties and drawstrings; lacing and eyelets; Velcro; snap fastenings such as poppers and press-studs; and buckles. You may find more of these or be able to make or adapt your own fastenings by taking them from existing items.

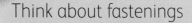

WORKOUT 83

Think about fastenings

Using a basic sportswear jacket shape – which is essentially a rectangle – start to add in different types of fastenings. Sportswear is particularly suitable for this exercise, and especially waterproof jackets of the sailing or climbing variety. These frequently have different types of fastenings on each pocket or pair of pockets.

Try to use a minimum of five different types of fastening.

START SIMPLE
This is a very simple sportswear jacket with a drawstring hood and concealed zip front placket. You can use this as a template for your task if you wish.

To increase the number of fastenings you can add a hood to the garment.

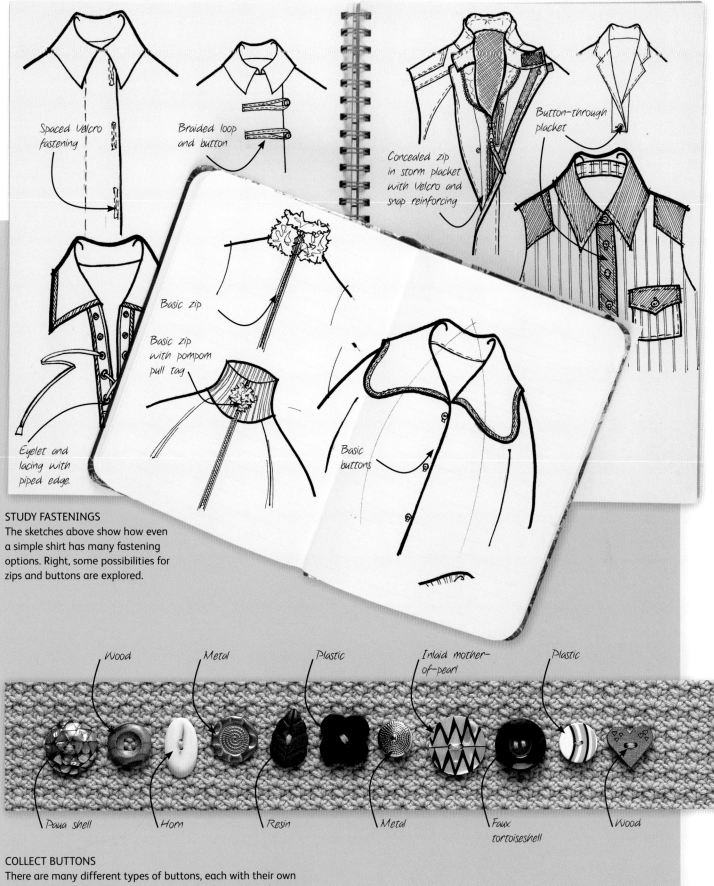

STUDY FASTENINGS
The sketches above show how even a simple shirt has many fastening options. Right, some possibilities for zips and buttons are explored.

COLLECT BUTTONS
There are many different types of buttons, each with their own distinct personality that can convey an inspiration. Your choice can make or break a garment. Start a collection of interesting buttons that you come across on old garments.

Preliminary sketches

Later in your career you will present preliminary sketches to a buyer you hope to impress, but for now they are a good design tool.

Preliminary sketches should be reasonably accurate, especially in proportion and detail, but they are not finished illustrations. They can take the form of black-and-white line drawings, with colour and fabric indications alongside, though it is preferable to have them coloured in.

Preliminary sketches are made in a layout pad, which is incredibly easy to use. The pages of the pad are made from very thin paper that acts like tracing paper.

Start sketching

Using the images above as a guide, try this with your designs. Start with something basic, then go on to adjust the silhouette. Add in details such as different pockets or collars.

You can fill dozens of layout pads just by making small changes each time.

■ **Don't forget** that making small changes allows you to evaluate your designs against each other when you view them later.

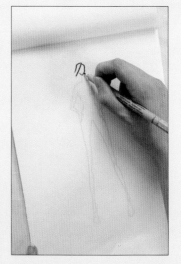

1 Starting at the back of the layout pad, place one of your figure drawings (see pages 44–45) between the backboard and the last page.

2 Line up the edges of the paper to position your figure centrally. Make sure that you can see the complete figure. Hold the page down firmly so that the figure does not move or become distorted.

3 Trace a copy of the figure onto the page. It is the convention to work in letter size and to make a single drawing on each sheet.

VARY THE THEME
Here are examples of preliminary sketches selected from many hundreds that show how the theme has developed. Note how frills and ruffs have been moved around the body and how the silhouette has subsequently changed.

WORKOUT 84

4 On the next page, draw a blank garment silhouette over the image of the figure. This garment should be one of the most important in the collection, but don't worry if it doesn't look right just yet.

5 You now need to redraw the garment, each time on a new page, adjusting the volume, fit, length, sleeves, and any other structural elements.

6 When you have achieved a silhouette you are happy with, you can add in the details. You will be able to see the silhouette under each new page.

7 On each new drawing, vary the design, placement, and scale of the details. Each single drawing counts as a new design and you will be amazed by how many of these you accrue.

Building your collection

A collection is a series of related garments, repeating fabric, style, and colour details. "Collection" is a designer's term, whereas a "range" tends to be a more commercial reference to the same thing. "Building a collection" refers to the process of editing down dozens of preliminary sketches and sketchbook work into a core set of around six to eight key pieces.

WORKOUT
85

Select your collection

You will need a lot of space for this workout, either on a wall or a floor. Lay out all of your designs and pick out the ones that you think are the best and would like to include in your collection. Remember to evaluate your choices in relation to all of your previous research. Think about your customer. It may help to make a "customer board" about them if you haven't already (see workout 28). Would they actually want to wear the outfit? Now go through your designs and pick out ten to twenty of your strongest ideas. Make sure that the collection makes sense, for example, if it is an autumn/ winter collection, does it have at least one heavy coat? And is it possible to make the garments you have chosen?

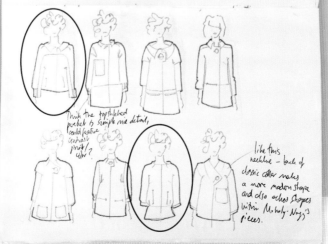

MAKE FIRST CHOICES
Pick your best designs at this stage. You can always rethink colours or fabrics or repeat details to bring them together into a coherent collection later.

ELIMINATE IDEAS
Narrow your selection. Here, the student has narrowed down a range of coat ideas because a small collection will typically only include one item of outerwear.

Bring it together

Go through your collection, referring back to your design drawings, choosing the strongest design details, and drawing them into the garments in your initial selection. Repeat this exercise with colour and fabric choices, ensuring that you use main and highlight colour and fabric combinations. Make design boards for each single outfit. To do this, present an illustration of each outfit on a piece of letter-sized card together with fabric swatches and working drawings. There are some good examples of design boards at the bottom of page 103.

There are some good examples of design boards at the bottom of page 103.

WORKOUT 86

This collection is based on stone and fire, which give a limited colour palette that has been spread throughout the collection. The checks have been repeated on the bottom half of all the outfits. Including short and long trousers creates flexibility, as does the inclusion of casual T-shirts and smarter shirts in the collection.

When using colour, make sure there is a "rhythm" in the collection. Use it in different scales and percentages, different placements on the body, in knit and in woven fabrics, and in solids, prints, and accents. This colour palette uses purples and greys with gold highlights.

WORKOUT 87

Balance your collection

You need to make sure your collection is balanced in terms of the type of garments you are offering. As a general rule, there should be three top garments designed for every one bottom item, although in summer this could go up to four to one. Think about "one-stop shopping" – you want to sell your customer all your looks, so avoid redundancy and make sure they don't have to go elsewhere for a skirt or a coat, for example. Edit your collection to your final six to eight key pieces.

This well-balanced collection shows a variety of garments, including dresses, tops, skirts, and trousers in a variety of fabrics, both plain and printed. Black has been used as an accent colour, but also appears in each outfit, thus binding the collection together.

This collection shows flat drawings with fabric swatches attached to them. Design details (such as the elaborate button placket with covered buttons and the pin tucks) have been repeated throughout the collection. A selection of trousers, dresses, and tops balances the collection.

Prints are used very well in this casual collection. The prints are of differing types, some quite dense and large-scale, others small-scale and revealing lots of white background. The collection combines jersey and woven fabrics, giving it a wearable, everyday feel. The silhouette has also been kept very simple with leggings or short trousers on the bottom teamed with a range of simple tops.

**WORKOUT
88**

Create a line-up

The line-up is the documentation of your collection that you will refer to all the time once you finally start to make the clothes. To make a line-up, take a piece of tabloid-sized board, photocopy the six to eight outfit designs you have selected as your best, and cut them out. Paste them onto the board. You must ensure that the design drawings are coloured and have fabric samples next to them where appropriate, because you are using the line-up to check for the balance of colours, fabrics, proportions, and details.

This garment shows the use of pleating that has been bound into the edge. Note the supporting strap that runs around the whole of the garment.

Pleating is used in tiers to add volume and movement to this garment. The simple undergarment provides a level of modesty, as the outer garment has been intricately cut around the bust.

Attach fabric samples that match with your final collection palette. Here, greys and silvers build on the "Silver Sixties" name.

COMPLETE THE LINE-UP

The line-up uses a more illustrative technique than your design drawings and presents a finished version of the collection. This collection was designed for the spring/summer season and is called "Silver Sixties".

This garment references the 1920s with layers of pleating and a simple A-line silhouette. The garment has again been cut to reveal décolleté.

This outfit shows a jacket to match the dresses and continues to use the pleated fabric as side panels and for the collar.

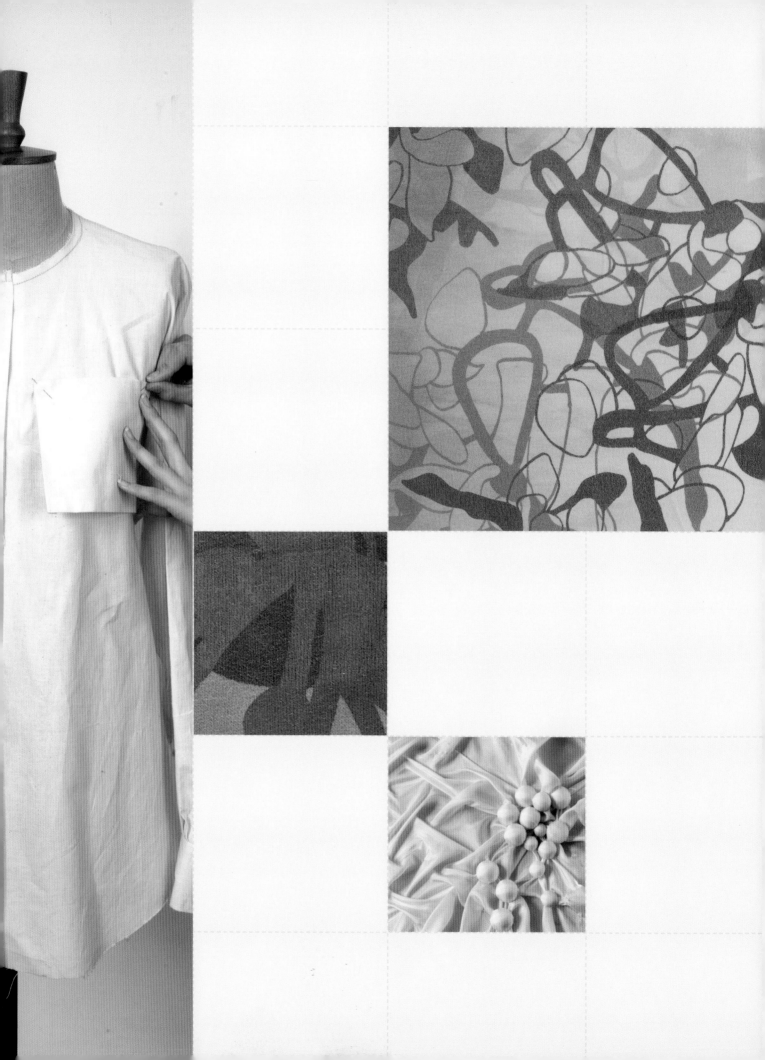

Chapter three:
Making

These workouts show you how you can design using 3D techniques, such as toiling, and how these processes lead to a final garment. Alternatively, create new looks from old by adapting and changing garments in as many ways as you can, using the workouts on customizing.

Draping

Draping and toiling (see pages 80–87) are ways of designing in 3D before you make a final paper pattern. Some designers pattern draft the rough idea, then finish it on the stand using the toiling process (see pages 80–87); others drape first and then commit to pattern (here). Try both as they challenge you in different ways. You can drape in your final fabric or a cheap alternative such as calico.

Preparing calico

WORKOUT 89

Calico needs to be "blocked" before any draping or toiling begins. Cut the fabric in a rectangle and iron it into a perfect "block" of 90 degree angles. Mark grain lines on the blocked calico (see workout 94). When you begin to work, make sure that the centre front and centre back match up with your grain line. Garments not cut properly "on grain" will twist and deform over time.

Learn about fabric

WORKOUT 90

Understanding fabric is an important part of being a successful fashion designer. Try generating ideas three-dimensionally, using a dress stand. Whenever possible, spend some time draping the actual fabric you intend to work with on the stand before you begin designing. Use dressmaker's pins to hold the fabric in place. Learn about how it hangs, its stretch, weight, and texture.

Take the most successful ideas from this research and experiment with them. Record your ideas as you progress, using your digital camera or a sketchbook. You will build a bank of ideas that you will be able to draw upon later in the design process.

RECORD THE DETAILS
By recording interesting details you may begin to think about where else they might be used on a garment and what else they could turn into. Perhaps you will have an idea for a collar, a hem detail, or a pocket? Here, for example, the designer has recorded a detail of the shoulder pleating.

Designing on a dress stand

Generating ideas directly by working on the dress stand will help you to visualize and consider scale, the drape of different fabrics, and the three-dimensional human form. Working in this way is a trial-and-error process, and often the best results are achieved accidentally. Record your work by drawing or photographing from all angles. When you are happy with the shape, you can sew it together to create the final garment.

1 When you are handling fabrics, it's important to work on surfaces that are clean and free from clutter. You might start with an unresolved idea in mind. Here, the designer is looking to create an exaggerated silhouette by using a layer of wadding under the main fabric.

2 Begin pinning your fabric to the dress stand. Drape, fold, and wrap the fabric into shape, pinning it into place as you go.

3 Pinning and creating drapes will help you to understand your fabric's strengths and possible weaknesses, as well as generate ideas for designs. Don't be afraid to take out pins and let your design evolve, but make sure you take notes as you go.

4 Intricate work requires care, time, and thought. As you develop your ideas you will naturally begin to edit and focus on the best ones. Once you are happy with your design, you can sew the drapes and folds in place to create the final garment.

Toiling

Like draping (see pages 78–79), toiling is a method of designing in 3D. The toile is a facsimile of your final garment made in cheap fabric and is used to test everything you have designed on paper. The fabric you toile with must be of a similar weight and have the same drape qualities as your final fabric. For example, if your final fabric is jersey, you will need to use a similar weight jersey for toiling. You may wish to refer to the Sewing Techniques chapter (pages 108–119) throughout the following workouts.

WORKOUT 92

Begin the toiling process

The first step in this process is to choose the design you want to develop into a toile. The following workouts will then take you through the toiling process outlined below.

The most common way of starting to toile is by adapting a suitable shop-bought pattern. You can cut around it fairly loosely, adding on extra fabric for length and volume if you wish to. If your garment is symmetrical, it is normal to make only one side of the toile, but for asymmetrical designs you will need to construct the whole garment.

Start toiling on a dress stand making adjustments as your toile develops by adding and removing dressmaker's pins. If you cut fabric off the toile it cannot be easily put back on, so try to stick to just using pins. Don't be disheartened if it doesn't look right immediately – you will find that you make many toiles before you reach the correct shape.

Each time you make an adjustment, take a photograph – you will be able to put these in your sketchbook later. Also, if you note why you changed the toile, you will find this helps you immensely in future.

When you are satisfied with your toile, you will need to transfer the whole thing to a piece of pattern paper, which will become your final pattern.

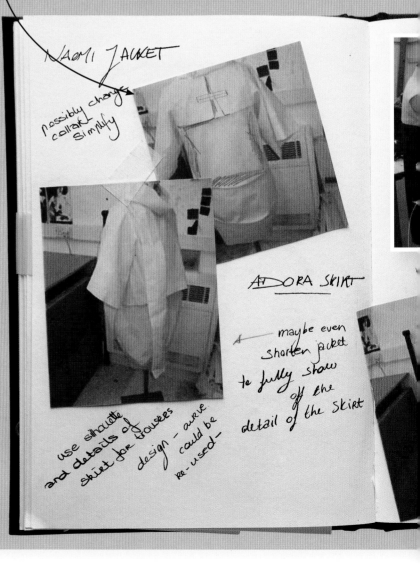

This sketchbook contains notes on the toiling process. The photos indicate how the garment will hang, and how the volume of fabric has been used. The toiles have been related to the original sketches and mood board to continually check whether the "feel" of the work is correct. One image shows two toiles together, which if you are able to do, gives a great indication of how your collection is developing.

NAOMI JACKET

possibly change collar simplify

ADORA SKIRT

maybe even shorten jacket to fully show off the detail of the skirt

use silhouette and details of skirt for trousers — design curve could be re-used —

In these developmental stages of a toile, the first shows the collar shape and how it will be attached, the second the starting point for the back. It is very important always to consider what happens on the back of a garment.

's Parisian / African culture

uette of outfit needs — too much volume the jacket needs to be more fitted to be balance out the volume...

...of the skirt

WORKOUT 93

Find a pattern

Choose a pattern that has the same basic silhouette as the design you want to toile. Check for length, shape of the shoulders, neck shape, and particularly the shape around the torso. Vintage patterns, like the one shown here, can be useful.

If you need to alter the length of the pattern, do so at this stage. Add length to the pattern equally all the way round to reflect the length depicted in your drawing. Do not change the neck and armholes.

To illustrate how you would put together a toile, the workouts on the following pages use this basic shop-bought pattern in conjunction with the design drawing you have chosen to toile.

WORKOUT 94

Learn pattern notation

Every pattern cutter has their own way of annotating a pattern but there are universal notations that everyone adheres to. Find these elements on your store-bought pattern and learn them.

- A solid border line is a cutting line.

- A dotted line is a stitching line (or seam-allowance line), normally 1.5 cm (⅝ in.) inside the cutting line.

- A grain line, or double-pointed arrow, indicates the direction of the grain of a woven fabric. The grain is parallel to the selvedge (the non-fraying edge). Some patterns need to be cut on the bias – at 45 degrees to the grain line.

- An arrow curving to the edge of a pattern indicates that this must be placed on a fold along the grain line.

- Notches placed on the edges of pattern pieces allow panels to be matched accurately.

- Dots or large spots are used to show the positions of darts, pockets, zips, or other details. Buttons are marked with crosses, buttonholes with a short line.

- Directional arrows show the sewing direction.

- Two parallel lines show where to lengthen or shorten a garment.

- Solid vertical lines show important lines or folds.

Add flare

You can add flare – additional fabric – to just about any pattern and in just about any place. It is most commonly used on the hems of skirts, dresses, trousers, sleeves, and sometimes even on necklines. Look at the shop-bought pattern you have chosen (see previous page). It is similar to your original design, but maybe it does not have the amount of volume you require. Plan how you are going to add some flare, referring to your original design.

WORKOUT 95

Adapt a pattern

In the previous workout you decided where you wanted to add flare – now try adjusting your shop-bought pattern referring to the steps shown here. This shows how flare has been added to a skirt. Dot-and-cross pattern paper has been used, which helps ensure the centre front or grain of your pattern is drawn correctly, usually either parallel or at 90 degrees to the edge of the paper.

This skirt flares from the waistband.

DECIDE WHERE TO FLARE
Flare can be added to the hems of trousers and skirts, collars and waistbands, bust seams – in fact just about anywhere there is fabric tight to the body.

Flare has been added halfway down this skirt.

A flared frill makes a straight skirt more interesting.

Flare can be added to sleeves.

Here, flare gives extra fullness around the hips.

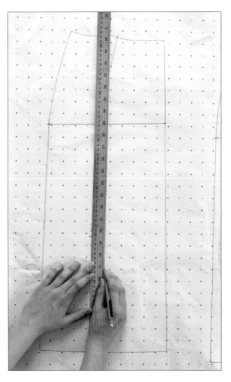

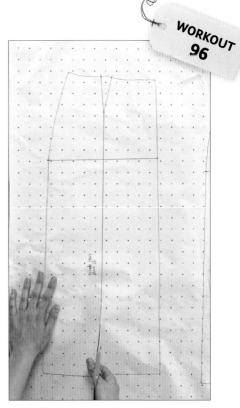

1 Draw the front of your basic shop-bought pattern onto pattern paper. Transfer any dots, notches, or other pattern notations carefully. Or you can add flare directly to your shop-bought pattern if you prefer.

2 Draw a vertical line, parallel to the centre front, from the hem of the garment to the bottom of the dart if there is one. Otherwise end your line about 7.5 cm (3 in.) from the top of the pattern piece.

3 Cut all the way around the pattern piece following the solid cutting line and then cut up the line you have drawn.

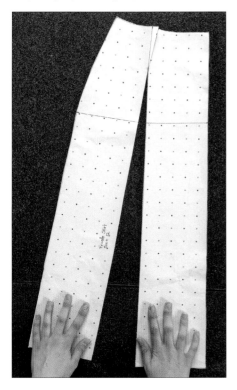

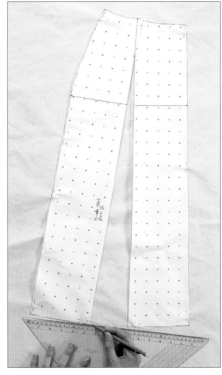

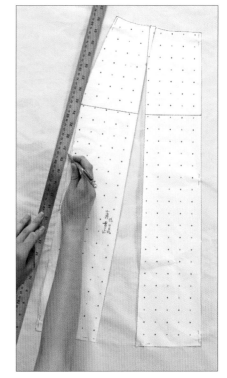

4 Spread out the paper where you have cut it. When you reach the width you require, fold down the excess that will have formed at the top of the pattern to form a new dart.

5 Transfer your flared pattern piece onto some plain pattern paper and pin it in place. With a ruler or other straight edge, draw in the hem.

6 Continue to draw around the flared pattern piece, transferring all the markings. You can add more flare to the sides of the pattern below the hip line if you wish.

WORKOUT
97

Cut your fabric

Whether you are cutting toiling fabric or final fabric, the method is the same. Place your fabric flat on a firm surface, with the right side facing up. Place your pattern pieces along the grain of the fabric and pin. Mark around the outer edge and the notches of the pattern pieces with tailor's chalk.

It is important to cut your fabric correctly, using very sharp scissors. Never use your fabric scissors for cutting paper or anything other than fabric because you will blunt them. Ensure you cut the notches and indicate any darts.

■ **Don't forget** to always cut with the pattern and garment on your right-hand side to ensure an accurate cut.

PIN THE PATTERN
Pin or weight the pattern carefully on top of the fabric. Use tailor's chalk to transfer any pattern markings onto your fabric.

CUT AROUND THE PATTERN
Carefully cut around the pattern, making sure the bottom blade of the scissors never leaves the table top. Keep your other hand behind the blades.

WORKOUT
98

Sew your toile

Sew the fabric pieces together to form your basic toile. First, match the seams using the notches, then pin the right sides together. Insert your pins at right angles to the seam as this allows the fabric to move through the sewing machine. Sew the seams using a basic straight stitch.

With a garment for the top half of the body, start with the shoulders. Move on to the centre front and back and/or side seams. Add the sleeves and then, finally, the collar if appropriate.

For a skirt, start with the side seams. Remember to add a fastening into the side seam at this point if needed (see pages 118–119). When you have completed this you are ready to attach the waistband (see page 116).

■ **Don't forget** that most bought patterns will provide an "order of work", advising you of the order in which the pieces should be sewn together.

SEW THE SEAMS
This student is using a professional flatbed sewing machine. These usually perform only one or two types of stitch, but they are more powerful than domestic machines.

Adjusting the toile

Toiling allows you to get to grips with the nature of fabric and make any necessary changes to your garment's design.

Fit your toile

You now need to view your toile on a model or dress stand and take photographs for future reference. Compare the silhouette against your original drawings. On tops, make sure the shoulders are not falling off, the neck is not too low or too high, and the length is correct. For a skirt or trousers, you need to be particularly aware of the positioning of the waistband in relation to the waist. Check the location of any pockets and whether it is easy to place your hands in them. Use pins to make adjustments, and take photographs of each stage.

CHECK THE TOILE
Does the toile look how you hoped? Does it fit and is it comfortable? This process may take several fittings and amendments, but it is worth persevering because it's important that it is correct.

Check the length

Look at your original drawing and check for proportion. For example, is the length of the garment correct, or is it too long?

The easiest way to check that the length is correct is to put your model or dress stand on a table and measure from the tabletop up to the hem with a long ruler. Measure all around the garment, and pin as appropriate.

DECIDE ON THE FINAL LENGTH
Marking your ruler with tape at the correct length will make it quick and easy to pin the garment at the same length all the way round.

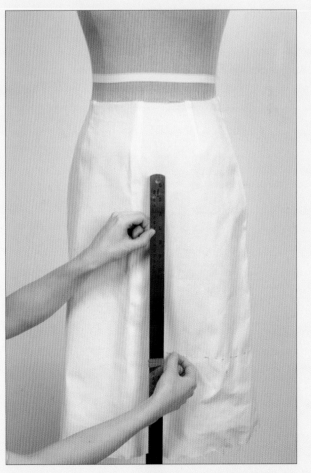

Check for too much volume

If your garment is too voluminous, you can add darts or increase the depth of existing darts (see page 112). You can also increase the seam allowance on your side seams. When making adjustments, ensure that they are carried out evenly, across the whole of the garment.

WORK INSIDE-OUT
Always adjust volume with the garment inside out so the seams and darts are easily accessible. Here, darts are being taken in, or increased in depth, to reduce the waist circumference.

Check for too little volume

If your garment is too tight, you will need to add additional fabric. This can be a trickier proposition than reducing the amount of volume. When doing this, remember that fabric has to be added evenly throughout the garment. Try reducing the darts (sometimes to nothing) and also reducing the seam allowances.

If this doesn't work, you will need to slash and spread your toile. Use a similar method to that shown in workout 96 for adding flare to a pattern – that is, cut up the centre of each section and pin in an extra panel of fabric to create the volume required. It is easier to do this on the actual toile first and then amend your paper pattern accordingly.

Add the details

When your toile is completed to your satisfaction, carefully draw on the position and the size of any simple details such as pockets, buttons, or embroidery. Once their position is marked, this information can be transferred to the final paper pattern. Toiles generally do not have finished pockets or linings or finished hems and seams.

ADJUST THE DETAILS
You can pin sample details on your toile. Here the designer is trying a sample of a patch pocket. You can then check the overall proportions of the pocket and its position on the garment.

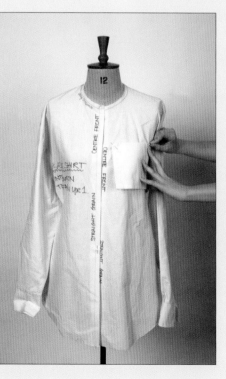

MEASURE FOR ACCURACY
Measure the details such as button spacing, ensuring each one is the same distance apart. Draw directly onto the toile.

Make up the finished garment

Once the toile is finished, mark notches on your toile at the hip and bust lines. Remove the toile from the stand, unpin it, and press it thoroughly (moving in the direction of the grain to prevent distortion). Now use the pressed toile to create your paper pattern, transferring the outline and all marks. On a flat, sturdy table, "true" the lines that will become the stitch lines, using rulers and curved rulers. Then add seam allowance, notches, darts, and any other notations.

Once you have adjusted your pattern, use it to recreate in your final fabric the garment you have toiled. Before cutting the fabric, make sure all grain lines run in the same direction.

Refer back to your shop-bought pattern to give you an idea of the correct order of construction. Sew as carefully as you can. If you have toiled and sampled everything beforehand, this should not be too difficult, and the pieces should go together smoothly.

When you have finished, you can compare your final garment with the toiles and sketches you produced along the way.

COMPARE CHANGES
On the far right, the final garment in burnt orange shows the changes made to the toile, shown on the right (detail below).

The finished neck edge has been neatly bound.

Smocking, buttons, and corded details have been repositioned.

The trousers have been made tighter and longer so they gather at the hem.

Customizing garments

Taking existing garments and customizing them is a much easier way of achieving a new look than starting from scratch, and can be just as effective. Customizing techniques are experimental and range from the very simple – such as dyeing the garment (see pages 92–93), or lengthening or shortening it – through to completely recutting a jacket or coat. Some of these tasks are similar in process to the toile fitting (see pages 80–87); however, it is still good to think about them afresh.

WORKOUT 105

Changing the proportions

The easiest way to adjust proportions is to play with length, either through shortening by cutting fabric away, though don't be too hasty about this, or lengthening by adding extra fabric onto the seams or hems. Alternatively, you could try wearing the garment lower or higher around the waist, which will make a significant difference to the proportions. Always check the results in a full-length mirror and photograph if appropriate.

Make simple changes

By making some simple changes to a pair of jeans you can create a completely new garment, namely a skirt. It is a good way to reinvent an old pair of jeans to freshen up your wardrobe for summer and it also is a great method of recycling.

1 Unpick the seams. Unpick just the inside leg, or, if you want a more voluminous skirt, also unpick the outside leg seam.

2 Try on the "skirt" and work out how long you want it to be. Cut to length.

3 Add triangular panels of fabric in denim (from the cut-off legs), or use another type of textile – as different as possible, such as tweed or leather.

Unpick the inside and outside leg seams.

WORKOUT 106

If you plan to do much deconstructing of denim, or any other garments, then a seam ripper is an awesome little device that allows you to rip quickly.

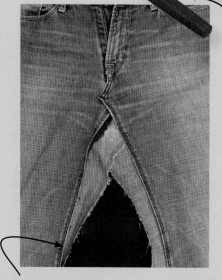

Use a sewing machine to attach extra triangular panels.

Deconstruct a garment

Here is an example of very complex customization. A pair of jeans has been completely cut up and turned into a denim jacket, using a shop-bought pattern. The end result will be a completely original design and a garment that feels very fresh compared with its shop-bought relations.

See how far you can take customizing using a shop-bought pattern. This works very well where the fabric of the original garment you cut up is not appropriate for the task you are using it for.

You can also go for very deconstructed looks, such as deliberately not making the garment well, using some of the fabrics the wrong way round, or leaving the seams on the outside.

TAKE IT FURTHER
With fabric used inside out, raw edges, and original stitching, this jacket has a very deconstructed look.

Alter the nature of the garment

Certain modifications can change a garment radically. Try removing the collar and replacing it with another from a similar sized item, but one that is different in nature – perhaps lace instead of plain shirting, or knitted instead of woven. You can also swap pockets or change buttons. If you feel really ambitious, you can change the sleeves, although this is a bit tricky.

FIND A STARTING POINT
Here, elements of a traditional four-pocket denim jacket (below) have been used with other garments and trims, to create the two new garments on the right.

The yoke, placket, hem, and two pockets from the original jacket have been added to a vintage blouse.

This variation is made from two jersey polka-dot tops combined with the denim collar, placket, side panels, and pockets.

Think about darts

WORKOUT **109**

The basic purpose of darts is very simple – it is to take fabric away so that the fit on the garment you are making is altered.

A dart is a triangle of fabric that has been taken away. To help you understand darts you can do this simple exercise. First, cut a circle of card. To make this into a cone, make one single cut from the circumference to the centre of the circle. Then overlap the two newly formed edges and a small cone will be formed. The more you overlap the edges the higher the cone becomes.

How could this cone relate to the body? What happens when you replace the cuts with folds? If you can answer these questions then you understand how darts function. Instructions for sewing darts can be found on page 112.

EXPERIMENT WITH DARTS
This sequence shows how a very large, shapeless garment can be altered to a more fitted shape. Darts have been added using pins and then sewn together.

Alter the cut

WORKOUT **110**

Take an oversized T-shirt and add darts to fit it into the body. The darts will reduce the amount of fabric volume, allowing less movement and making the silhouette narrower. They should be placed appropriately, which is usually around the waist and below the bust. However, you can put darts into just about any part of a garment, from the shoulders to the neck to the hem.

You can also alter the line of trousers, though it is much easier to make them narrower than it is to make them wider. This is achieved by resewing the inside and outside leg seams.

Use pins to form the darts so you can rearrange them easily.

The darts have dramatically altered the silhouette and added interesting style details.

Embellish fabric

Embellishment is the use of techniques and materials to enhance the surface of a fabric and add design interest. Keep a "treatment library" of images in your sketchbook. Go through magazines and rip out samples of embellishments, then look through these possibilities when designing. Take an old garment and freshen it up by using embellishments of your choice.

MIXED EMBELLISHMENT
Embroidery and beading over appliqué.

BEADING
Here, beading has been added over black knit. Note that the edge is finished with the same mock pearl beads.

APPLIQUÉ
This example uses several complementary fabric types including gingham, Liberty print floral, and a shirting stripe.

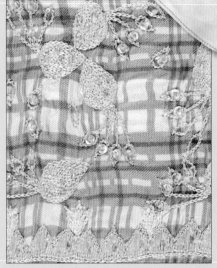

EMBROIDERY AND SEQUINS
This embroidery has been placed over a plaid fabric. The sequins have been used to enhance the floral design.

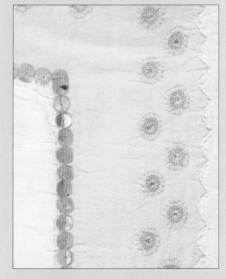

APPLIQUÉ, SEQUINS, AND EMBROIDERY
Embellishment often works well when there are many different processes and materials on the same sample. Here, this gives a feminine, transparent effect.

PRINT AND EMBELLISHMENT
This print has been specially designed for one part of the garment – a placement print. In addition, the figure has been picked out in sequins and beads.

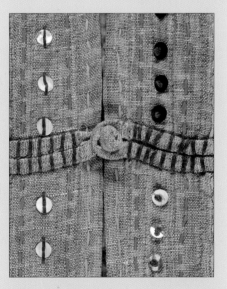

HAND EMBROIDERY
This embroidery has been done by hand rather than machine and allows for the use of a heavier embroidery thread. Sequins have been added to the final design.

Dyeing garments

Another customizing option is dyeing. Many garments can have their colour changed, which will dramatically alter their appearance. After using a bleach solution to remove existing colour, you can start thinking about how you are going to colour it. Do you want a solid dye treatment – one colour all over – or something with colour gradations? Do you want to mask out certain areas, as with tie-dyeing or batik? When you have decided on the technique, sample a small area and, if it is satisfactory, repeat it for the whole garment. If you follow the instructions from the dye manufacturer, generally you can't go wrong.

Changing colour: solid colour

WORKOUT 113

Dyeing is most successful when the fabric has not been treated, for example by being pre-dyed in a factory, or has had all colour removed. The best fabric to dye is "greige" fabric, which is unbleached and untreated, or other untreated white fabrics.

Natural fabrics are usually easier to dye than manmade fibres. Fabrics that are composed of more than one type of yarn can be problematic to dye evenly.

To achieve a solid colour, place your garment in a bucket or deep tray of dye, mixed following the manufacturer's instructions, and leave until it reaches the required colour.

■ **Don't forget** that different dyes will require different lengths of time to achieve the correct colour, so keep checking.

Remove all colour

WORKOUT 112

You will first need to bleach out the existing colour by immersing the garment in a 5 per cent bleach solution and leaving it overnight. You will need to agitate the garment occasionally, wearing gloves or using tongs. The garment is ready when it reaches an ecru state; this is a neutral, creamy colour.

Some fabrics are more suitable for bleaching than others: cottons are good, whereas Lycra-based and polyester garments may not bleach, and may even decay badly.

Remove some colour

Try dipping small areas of the garment in bleach or flicking bleach onto the fabric to create a splash effect. You can do this using a paintbrush or a toothbrush. Be careful of other clothes and furnishings; wear gloves and work in a well-ventilated area.

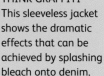

WORKOUT 114

THINK GRAFFITI
This sleeveless jacket shows the dramatic effects that can be achieved by splashing bleach onto denim.

WORKOUT 115

Change colour by dip-dyeing

You will most frequently use dip-dyeing on garments, colouring just the edges, such as the hems, cuffs, and collars, by dipping them into a bucket or tray of dye. Alternatively, you can spray dye onto your fabric with a spray bottle.

DIP-DYE DIFFERENT FABRICS
This crinkle organza has been dip-dyed twice. It also demonstrates how different fabrics react to dyes to give differing results.

CHANGE PATTERNED FABRICS
This fabric shows how a printed fabric can be dip-dyed successfully.

Change colour by tie-dyeing

Before you immerse your garment in your bucket of dye, mask off certain areas of your fabric. Traditional tie-dyeing involves tying pieces of fabric around a garment that has been twisted together to make it compact. However, you can also use string or thread to create finer lines of undyed fabric, or stitch on scraps of fabric to act in the same way.

WORKOUT 116

EXPERIMENT WITH DIFFERENT TIES
Here a rack of garments have all had various tie-dye treatments to create a huge range of patterns.

TRY SEVERAL COLOURS
More than one colour can be used to create interesting tie-dye effects. Bright colours are particularly effective.

Chapter four:
Styling & promotion

Fashion relies as much on the presentation of your ideas as the designs themselves. These workouts look at techniques to make your work feel professional and give you the confidence to start showing it to other people, from styling and photographing your work, to putting together an eye-catching and successful portfolio.

Styling

There are lots of different ideas about what styling is and what a stylist does. Styling involves the creation of new looks that are more forward-looking than current trends. It will involve using garments, accessories, hair and make-up, and, importantly, the right model.

Quite often, styled magazine photo shoots are centred around a theme. As with just about everything else in fashion, the best styling themes have absolutely nothing to do with contemporary fashion. The following exercises allow you to experiment with styling themes and try out a few ideas that will help you to present your clothes.

WORKOUT 118

Find inspiration

Choose an era of fashion, or look at an ethnic group's traditional dress. Try to choose something that you have already researched. Look into your chosen area more closely to find out more details about life in that time or place.

Using the ideas from your research based on the theme you have chosen, style your model appropriately. This works especially well if you also choose the correct location and assemble some appropriate props.

WORKOUT 117

Mix it up

Collect images of a group or subculture, such as punks or skaters. Or choose something less obvious, perhaps geishas, truckers, or hunters, for example. Work out what is specific to the group – what garments, make-up items, hairstyles, and accessories, such as shoes, belts, hats, sunglasses, and jewellery are used. Think about how these elements could be mixed with your collection without overwhelming it. It may help to think of a versatile celebrity, a supermodel for example, and consider how she would look wearing items from your chosen group. Collect pieces that could be worn successfully by both the group and the model, ready to use in your photo shoot.

IDENTIFY THE LOOK
The traditional geisha costume is highly stylized and specific. If you choose this as your theme, study it to identify all the elements that make up the look, from the shape of the sleeves and length of the garment, to the way it is worn, and the hair, make-up, and posture.

STYLING CHOICES
The job of a stylist is to create a total look. This outfit draws heavily on inspiration from the Indian subcontinent. The garment references the sari with its loose, draping effects and the textile is a traditional paisley woven design. The stylist has complemented this with heavy kohl around the eyes and an ethnic-inspired hairstyle.

Focus on the head

Concentrate your idea on the head area. Try out hairstyles and make-up ideas. Use runway imagery and previous research to generate interesting approaches to make-up. Use hairpieces and wigs, or try dyeing and cutting the model's hair (if they are willing) for more idiosyncratic looks.

WORKOUT 119

WORKOUT 120

Reinvent the runway

Choose a current runway collection and try to recreate the look using clothes that are accessible to you. Particularly concentrate on hair, make-up, and accessories.

WORKOUT 121

Layer garments

Dressing up your garments is the essence of styling, and a stylist will own a large assortment of clothing and accessories with which to do this. They will also supply the theme within which these accessories are applied in the photo shoot.

Dress your model in several layers of different clothing. Experiment with different ideas, such as putting something skintight over an oversized T-shirt. Try out a variety of lengths of hems and sleeves, and consider mixing sheer and solid fabrics, print and plain. Be innovative with the garments, and try them on in unusual ways, for example using the armhole as the neck opening or the sleeves as the legs.

■ **Don't forget** that a few bulldog clips, used out of sight of the camera, will come in useful when you want to alter the silhouette quickly.

VARY THE LOOK
A simple garment can be given a completely different feel if layered with other garments or combined with different accessories. Layering gives an outfit a strong identity, and attention to detail in accessories helps personalize the look.

Photo shoot

Now you have thought about how to style your finished designs, you need to consider how to photograph them. One of the most important ways that fashion labels are promoted and sold is through photographs in adverts, magazines, catalogues, and newspapers. The workouts here look at how to take good fashion photographs that provide the finishing touch to your designs. There is no need for professional equipment; your everyday digital camera will take photos good enough to use in your portfolio or post on a Web page. Before you begin, look back at the research you carried out into the theme you chose in the Getting Started chapter.

Choose a location

Take photographs of locations you think have potential for a fashion shoot and paste them into a book. Remember that weather conditions or the time of day can dramatically change a location. When you are planning a shoot, look through the photographs you have gathered and choose those that you think suit your styling. Draw or make a collage of the outfit(s) and any props onto the photographs as a way of testing locations.

WORKOUT 122

Choose a model

At this stage you probably won't be using a model agency, so you need to start your own book of models. Approach people you think would look good wearing your designs. At first, they will probably be friends and family. Take a photograph of your model's face and write down their dress size, height, and shoe size. Generally, fashion models are tall because the fabric hangs better on them. Make a note of what their face means to you, for example Pre-Raphaelite ethereal beauty, or tough and angular with attitude. When you are planning a shoot, pick out a model who suits your styling ideas. Try the outfit on your chosen model, and take some test shots to check you have got it right.

Name: Holly Lolle
Height: 5 ft 6 in. (167 c
Dress size: 8
Shoe size: 6 (5 in heels)
Hair colour: brown
Bust measurement: 32
Hip measurement: 34 i
Inside leg measuremen
Revealing clothes: No
Telephone number: 078

Name: Tracy Fitz (Holly L's cousin)
Height: 5 ft 7 in. (170 cm)
Dress size: 10
Shoe size: 7 (6 in heels)
Hair colour: brown
Bust measurement: 36 in. (92 cm)
Hip measurement: 36 in. (92 cm)
Inside leg measurement: 32 in. (82 cm)
Clothes: No

WORKOUT 124

WORK UP TO IT
Start with some simple, static poses before moving on to more complicated "action" poses or poses using props or multiple models. You might find that putting on some music will help your model to relax and move.

THINK ABOUT THE DETAILS
These images show two potential locations for a photo shoot. Think about how colourful you want your final image to be, how much background to include or edit out, whether you want to shoot at night or in daylight, and if you want there to be any movement or passers-by.

Photograph the model

Make sure the model is relaxed, their hair and make-up are perfect, the garment looks great, and the location and light are just right. Get the model to pull some faces and strike some poses while you check for composition on your camera's LCD screen. When everything is in place it's time to take the final photographs. Aim to take a mixture of long-distance and close-up photographs, particularly those that concentrate on the face, or other areas of detail, in contrast to full-length figures. You can also try rotating the camera 90 degrees to give yourself a mixture of landscape and portrait photographs.

KNOW WHAT YOU WANT
Show your model some images that you have pulled out of magazines to give them an idea of what you want, but make sure you don't put them off by being too demanding!

Select the image

Make an initial selection by printing out a contact sheet and putting a cross through unsuccessful images from corner to corner.

For the remaining images you will need to consider composition, colour, shape, and texture and whether, most importantly, the photographs achieve the desired look. You should select the images you feel are the most inventive. Consider including some strong silhouettes and close-ups of interesting details.

Remember, photo-editing software allows you to enhance an original image in a multitude of ways or transform an image into something different entirely.

Promotion

One of the most important aspects of fashion is the promotion of your designs, and many designers – and others – are employed solely to work in this area. Graphic design and marketing all make important contributions to this area of the fashion industry. These workouts look at the promotional materials that are associated with the production and retailing of a collection, and that provide the finishing touches to your designs.

First of all, you need to look back at the research you carried out in the Getting Started chapter, particularly paying attention to the research theme you chose.

WORKOUT 126

Brush Script Standard

Minion Pro

Hobo Standard

Futura Medium

Birch Standard

Label your collection

Decide on a name for your collection. Most designers choose to use their own name, though this is not always the case. Now think about how to make the name look good when printed or embroidered on a hang-tag or label. Use a word-processing software program to test out various typefaces. If the collection has a young and feminine feel, you may choose a script typeface that resembles handwriting. If design and structure are more important, you could choose a more geometric typeface, such as Futura. Try lots of different versions, then go for the one you are happiest with.

WORKOUT 127

Produce a hang-tag

The hang-tag is the card that hangs from a garment and gives the designer's name, sizing information, washing and care instructions, and information about the fabrics.

First of all decide on the colour scheme. You could have the same colours for every season, or you may choose to change the colours of the text and card according to your season's colours. Whatever you decide, always keep the same type and logo. Refer back to your colour story for this version.

Source some card in the colour of your choice and check that it will go through a photocopier or colour printer. Print your hang-tag information – whatever you have chosen to include – onto the card and attach it to the garment using embroidery thread in a matching colour and a very small safety pin.

LOOK AT TAGS
Hang-tags give practical information but can also reflect the mood and message of your collection.

WORKOUT 128

Producing a label

To make the label you will need to use a sewing machine that is capable of embroidery – some machines can be attached to scanners, which is even better. Scan in the artwork for your logo, or find a similar typeface on your sewing machine. Embroider onto a piece of ribbon of an appropriate colour and you have an instant label.

Preparing your portfolio

Your portfolio is the body of work you carry to an interview, whether for a position within the industry or for a course in education. It represents the sum of all the work you have undertaken so far and should illustrate your interests in the subject area and the ways in which you think through problems. It is important to show complete projects from initial idea to finished article. You should include a full range of your ideas and show as many processes and skills as possible.

WORKOUT 129

Select work for an interview for a course

The goal of the portfolio is to flaunt your talent and your abilities and show your passion for fashion. An ideal fashion portfolio will contain six or seven collections: three autumn/winter, three spring/summer, and one other, for example, accessories or swimwear. The groups should have varied colour stories and inspirations, but all be for one focused customer.

Consider having illustrated collections, as well as CAD work, and textile design. Photographs of 3D work will enrich the portfolio's "texture" and shows you can realize your designs.

You should also include a separate sketchbook that shows the evolution of thought, motif filtration, and process. If your existing sketchbooks don't do this, rework them into a more structured format.

It is important to show other skills in a portfolio, particularly for schools that have a "foundation year". Basic fine-art skills are essential – painting, drawing, figure work, and drawing from observation.

This spread demonstrates how 3D work can be incorporated into your portfolio. It shows toile development combined with fabric swatches and inspirational imagery.

These are excellent examples of what portfolio sketchbook pages should look like. They are lively, full of ideas, with clear reference to the starting point and strong design direction leading from this.

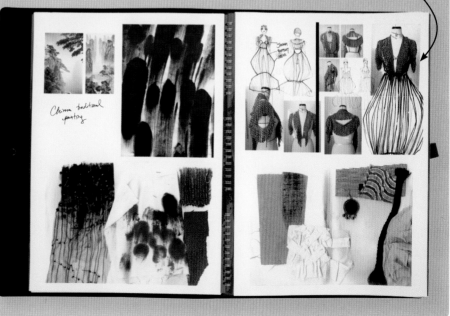

Choose your best sketchbook pages

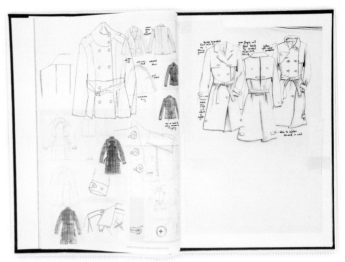

Here the designer illustrates the theme and links this to initial samples, and so shows how the idea is developing. The theme here is glamorous travel from bygone eras.

On these pages, the designer has highlighted a particular garment – the trench coat – and is starting to think about what constitutes such a garment and how changing small details could update this classic.

Initial sketches show how the designer is starting to think about print placement on simple dress shapes. Fabric samples and yarn cards stem from the initial research.

Here the designer is starting to think of fabrics, colours, and design details that can be used with the basic trench coat shape. A loose illustrative device breaks up the visuals, to avoid a repetitious feel.

This spread is a version of some final illustrations and fabric swatches, using CAD. There are subtle references to the theme in the background. Typed notes help explain the designs.

Show you understand your customer

Here is a good example of a customer board that clearly identifies the type of person the designer would wish to be wearing the clothes. This is reinforced by placing the figure in a period interior scene and overlaying faux Victorian trim and miniature gilt picture frames to provide further atmosphere.

This more commercial customer board shows intelligent, design-led young women who are progressing into adulthood. The layout is clean, precise, and considered, reflecting the feel of the collection.

Impress with your designs

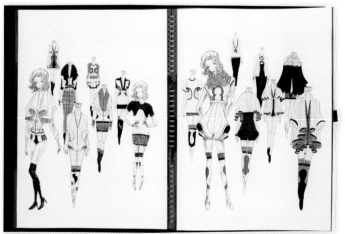

The purpose of the line-up in a portfolio is to show a significant proportion of the designer's range on one board. It is usually made up of a series of images of between six and eight outfits. It differs from design boards in that working drawings and detailed descriptions are not included.

Yarn swatches have been used as colour information on this design board for Levi's. Note the board's uncluttered look, which makes the design concept clear.

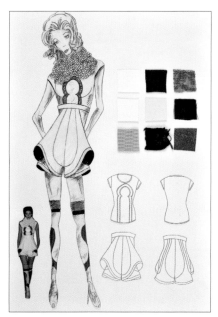

This design board shows a design illustration, working drawings, a photo of the finished garments, and fabric swatches. The designer has chosen not to add text, though normally this would be expected.

Present the finished garments

RACHEL FONG

The urban setting of these shots reflects the feel of the garments. The action poses identify them as being for a younger market.

If you have had a runway show, make sure someone photographs it (the designer is always backstage!) as this will provide an invaluable record of your work.

Other skills you could showcase

A bold collage for a summer outfit, using the designer's own fabric designs.

A very well-executed observational life drawing of a man's head.

This detailed pencil sketch is used instead of photography and supplies more visual interest for the viewer.

A very strong collage illustrating an outfit the designer would like to make in future. The use of fabric and a lovely colour palette have created a feeling of comfort and warmth in keeping with an autumn/winter design.

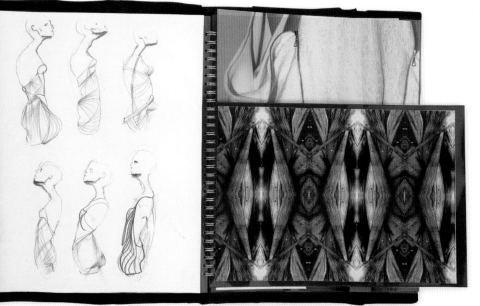

Some elegant sketches showing design development related to the original theme.

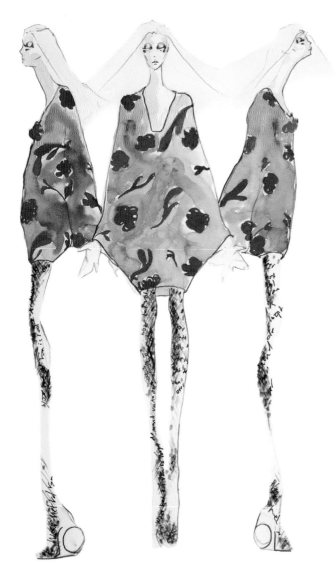

This delicate sketch works well because it shows the obvious front view but offers side views of the dress as well. The competent watercolour technique helps define the texture and volume of the garment.

Using CAD

Computer-aided design is a powerful tool, and as a young fashion designer you will be expected to master it. Traditional design and drawing is important, too, but you should include some strong examples of CAD work in your portfolio, such as this polished line-up.

What makes a winning portfolio?

Follow the rules for portfolio submissions as outlined in your college catalogue, admissions office, or online resources.

1 Make it visually strong. Start with a bang and end with a bang!

2 Don't include artwork that is over one year old. Your collection should be your most recent work.

3 You may be asked to choose a limited number of pieces. Be selective. Make it your best work. If in doubt, don't include it.

4 Your work may include lots of varied pieces. Think about how you want them ordered. Decide on a theme or context and run through it with a friend or teacher to see what they think.

5 Your work might explore (and show how you approached) a given subject. It might outline how you responded to a certain theme in a personal way. This research should inform the development of your ideas. Keep a journal critiquing your work as it progresses. The entire portfolio should be underpinned by thorough and wide-ranging research about the subject in the form of sketchbooks, journals, photography, and even relevant ephemera.

Use these guidelines to edit your work.

- Are there many similar pieces in your portfolio already? If so, edit them down.

- Is your portfolio inventive? Don't copy material or mimic the styles of other artists.

- Does it show a process of thinking?

- Are you demonstrating a particular set of skills, such as a fantastic drawing ability, an interest in fabrics or silhouette, or perhaps simply passion and a wide range of basic skills?

- Does your personality and the way you express yourself visually shine through in the portfolio?

- Don't take yourself too seriously. Show you have a sense of humour.

- Is your portfolio aesthetically pleasing? Does it challenge perceptions? Is it full of surprises?

In an increasingly technology-based world, portfolios that show good observational skills in drawing are popular. Instructors are not looking for fully rounded mini-professionals but for applicants who show promise.

Presenting your work

The way in which you present your work is as important as the work itself. Your presentation file should make it easy to decipher your ideas and intentions, and should be clean and edited down to a manageable format.

You will need some specialist equipment to make your work look really good, including a portfolio to carry it in.

Choose a portfolio

WORKOUT 130

Decide on the size of portfolio you want to work with. The standard in industry is A4, although when you are starting out in your career and trying to show more ideas you will probably use a larger portfolio size. When you have arrived at the correct size, sort through your work and make sure it will fit in the portfolio.

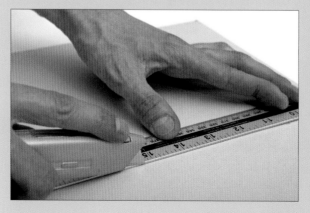

Include a range of work in your portfolio, to show the development of your ideas.

Use multiple mounts

WORKOUT 131

One of the most effective ways of displaying your work is to mount a few images or examples of it onto one large piece of card. Choose similar pieces, usually from the same project, and arrange them on the card, moving them around until you are satisfied with the composition. Then mount the work with "simple mounting" (see workout 134).

Trim your work

WORKOUT 132

If the edges of your work are damaged, or the paper is not the size you require, use a sharp craft knife and a metal ruler to trim the images neatly. When using a craft knife, make sure you keep the ruler flat and on a solid surface suitable for cutting on.

TAKE IT SLOWLY
When cutting with a craft knife, don't press down heavily on the blade in an attempt to slice through the card in one go. Draw the blade along the edge of the ruler to make a light initial cut, then keep cutting along the same groove until you have sliced through the card.

Mount your work: window mounting

You can buy special equipment to do this, although similar results can be achieved with a sharp blade and careful measuring. Take care with window mounting, because using too much of it and with the wrong imagery could do your work an injustice.

THE RIGHT TOOL
This window-mounting tool makes a neat 45-degree cut.

Mount your work: simple mounting

Choose good-quality black or white card – whatever anyone tells you, any other colour will make your work look as if it were produced at school. Spray some repositioning glue from a short distance away onto the back of the image you wish to mount, and position it centrally on the card. Ensure that there is more "space" or excess card below the image.

■ **Don't forget** to lightly mark the centre of the image you are mounting and line it up with a central mark you have made on the card.

Include a CV

You should always include a CV with your portfolio. This will often change with each interview, and should reflect your skills in the same way that the portfolio does.

Choose an appropriate typeface. Remember that this is a design project (even if graphic design rather than fashion design).

You need to include your name and contact details, educational experience and qualifications, and employment history, including work experience. Include a section on skills, since qualities such as working as part of a team are often as important as subject-specific skills. Also include a small personal statement about your unique selling points.

Present yourself for an interview

Some fashion schools like to interview applicants. If you get invited for an interview at a fashion school, you might consider wearing one of your own creations. If not, then you should still dress to show your interest in clothes and fashion.

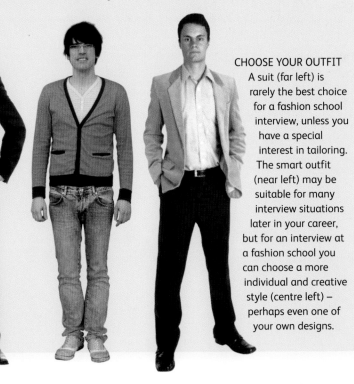

CHOOSE YOUR OUTFIT
A suit (far left) is rarely the best choice for a fashion school interview, unless you have a special interest in tailoring. The smart outfit (near left) may be suitable for many interview situations later in your career, but for an interview at a fashion school you can choose a more individual and creative style (centre left) – perhaps even one of your own designs.

Chapter five:

Sewing techniques

Fashion ultimately relies on making garments with a professional finish. Use these workouts as a short course in basic sewing, or just dip into them when you need to. They will teach you the basic processes required to start constructing finished garments that you have designed yourself.

Let's get sewing

There are some basic sewing skills you will need to learn if you are to complete some of the tasks in this book. As with drawing skills, your sewing will only improve if you practise, so don't expect to get it right first time. For the following sewing workouts you will need your sewing machine and thread, iron and ironing board, and pieces of plain fabric about 25 x 50 cm (10 x 20 in.). For some of the later workouts you may need some old garments to practise on.

WORKOUT 137: PRACTISE BASIC SEWING

Get used to your sewing machine by practising lines of the following basic sewing.

1 Adjust the stitch length depending on the fabric – lengthen it for thicker fabric and shorten it for finer material.

2 On stretch fabrics, use a narrow zigzag stitch or a stretch stitch, or the threads may break as the seam gets pulled during wear.

3 Check the tension. If the bobbin thread shows on the top, the tension is too tight. If the top thread loops through to the underside then the tension is too loose.

WORKOUT 138: LEARN HOW TO PRESS

Careful pressing is key to constructing a garment.

Use a pressing cloth to protect the surface of fabrics. Silk organza is ideal. When pressing a seam, first press it flat, then open it from the wrong side, and finally hover the iron over the right side (with a pressing cloth if necessary). To prevent ridges forming on the right side, place thin card stock between the fabric and seam allowances.

Seams and hems

A seam is a means of joining two pieces of fabric. Choose the most appropriate method considering the fabric type and the position of the seam within the garment you are making. Hems on the lower edge of garments need to be finished so they are straight and level.

WORKOUT 139: SEW A PLAIN SEAM

This is the simplest method of joining two pieces of fabric. Use it for straight or curved seams and all materials. Choose an appropriate seam allowance, usually 1.5 cm (⅝ in.). On curved seams, snip or clip into the seam allowance so the fabric lies flat. On stretch fabric, use a twin needle and fit a walking foot. This prevents the fabric from puckering and gives some stretch to the hem. The resulting hem has a professional finish.

1 Place the right sides together, matching the raw edges, and pin along the sewing line.

Use a straight stitch and sew along the sewing line, removing the pins as you go.

3 Press the seam open or to one side and neaten using a seam finish.

Workout 140: Make a double-folded hem

A double-folded hem is folded twice to conceal the raw edges within. It may be wide or narrow, and finished by hand or with machine topstitching. Use it on woven and knitted fabrics to provide a neatly finished edge on shirts, blouses, T-shirts, and trousers. If the hem is curved, tucks will form when the raw edge is folded up. To minimize this, make a curved hem very narrow.

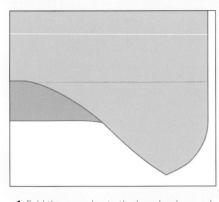

1 Fold the raw edge to the hem level around the circumference of the hem.

2 Fold up again to conceal the raw edge at hem level and pin to hold it in place.

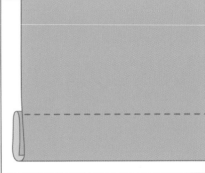

3 Neatly sew the hem by hand (see below) or with machine topstitching.

Workout 141: Do a ROLLED HEM

A rolled hem is a narrow, finished edge, which is useful on lightweight and sheer fabrics such as chiffons and silks. It can be sewn by hand, or using a sewing machine.

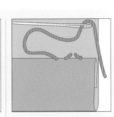

Machine a line of straight stitching just below the hem level and trim very close. Attach a rolled-hem foot to the sewing machine and feed the stitched edge into the foot. Guide the fabric edge as the foot feeds the fold under the needle and stitches it in place. To sew by hand, roll the edge with your thumb and first finger and hold the roll in place with small slip stitches.

Workout 142: Do a HAND-FINISHED HEM

A hand-sewn hem is the best option where stitches should not be visible on the right side. Hem stitch, slip stitch, herringbone stitch, and lockstitch are all useful, and your choice of one of them will depend on the type and weight of your fabric as well as your personal preference. A hand-stitched hem isn't as strong as a machined one, but the stitches will be invisible.

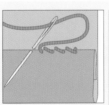

Hem stitch
Use hem stitch where a strong finish is required, such as on medium- to heavy-weight fabric.

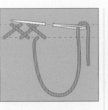

Slip stitch
This method is less visible than hem stitch, so it is suitable for fine material. For a good result, keep the stitches well spaced, yet even. Always use a thread in a closely matching shade.

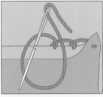

Herringbone stitch
This stitch is suitable for both medium- and heavyweight stretch fabrics since the stitches "give" if the hem is pulled.

Lockstitch
Thread loops around each stitch in a lockstitched hem. This means that if the thread breaks, the hem will not unravel fully. Keep the stitches well spaced and even. This is a suitable method for all fabric weights.

Darts

A dart allows for shaping to be introduced into a garment. Darts are ideal for removing excess fabric at the waist of slacks or skirts, or at the bust of a garment. It's often necessary to snip into the dart to allow it to lie flat. Press either to the centre or to the side seams, but be consistent throughout the garment.

WORKOUT 143: SEW A SINGLE-POINTED DART

Darts are formed with a gently curved line of stitching. Practise marking darts accurately and sewing a smooth curve. Try pressing both to the centre and to the side and consider if you need to snip the dart so it lies flat.

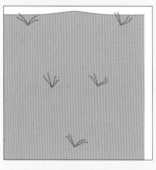   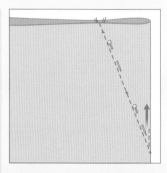

1 Transfer pattern markings before removing the pattern from the material. Use tailor's tacks, chalk, or wash- or fade-away pens.

2 Fold the fabric through the point of the dart and match up the markings on the edge with the right sides together. Pin together along the marked line.

3 Starting from the edge, stitch towards the point in a smooth, gentle curve.

4 Secure thread ends by reverse stitching into the body of the dart or by hand sewing.

WORKOUT 144: SEW A DOUBLE-POINTED DART

This type of dart has a point at each end and is generally used around the waist area on dresses, jackets, or coats, to create a smooth shape. It's possible to start at one point and sew to the other, but the method shown here gives a neat finish and the centre threads lock each other in place. Practise sewing and pressing a double-pointed dart.

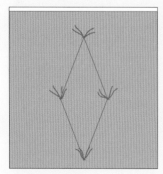 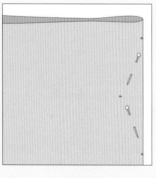  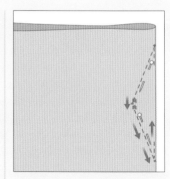

1 Transfer pattern markings accurately before removing the pattern from the material.

2 With right sides together, fold the fabric through the points of the dart and match the pattern markings between them. Pin and/or tack (stitch loosely) together.

3 For a neat and secure finish, start at the middle and sew a smooth curve to one point. Secure the thread ends.

4 To sew the other half of the dart, turn the garment, sew over four or five stitches and then continue to the other point. Finish as before.

Pleats

Pleats are clever folds of fabric used in a variety of ways to reduce excess fabric in a specific place and to control fullness, or add style. They may be soft or sharp, but must be accurately measured to look good.

WORKOUT 146: SEW BOX PLEATS

A box pleat is a reversed inverted pleat (see right). The two folds face away from each other on the surface giving a wide vertical pleat. Use it on skirts, pockets, and the centre back of a shirt where it meets the yoke. Box pleats may be stitched partly down, or left to hang free from the waist or a seam. Choose the fabric wisely. Synthetic fabrics may be too springy, while natural fabrics may pleat well, but also crease badly. Practise marking, pressing, and sewing box pleats using the same method shown for inverted pleats (right) but, in step 2, fold the pleat with the wrong sides of the cloth facing.

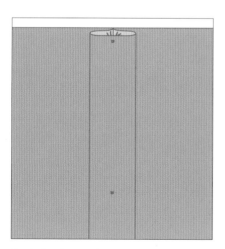

Stitch the pleat in place and press, then fold so the centre seam lies flat and directly below the centre of the box pleat.

WORKOUT 145: SEW INVERTED PLEATS

Pleats can be stitched down or left to hang free from a seam or waistband, and be either soft or pressed crisply. An inverted pleat consists of two folds that face each other. Use inverted pleats in skirts, pockets, and the yokes of blouses and dresses. For best results, choose a fabric that will hold the pleat's shape. If stitched down, reverse over the end stitches to finish and secure the pleat. Practice marking, pressing, and sewing inverted pleats.

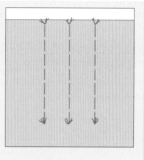

1 Mark the position and size of the pleat with tailor's tacks or chalk (on the wrong side of the fabric).

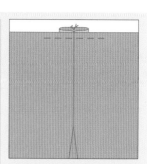

3 Press the line of stitching and fold so the centre crease lies directly below the seam. Tack within the seam allowance.

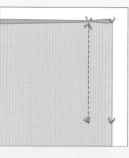

2 Fold the pleat through the centre with the right sides of the cloth facing. Machine a straight stitch along the marked line.

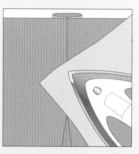

4 Press the inverted pleat using a cloth to protect the surface, and continue with the next pleat.

WORKOUT 147: SEW KNIFE PLEATS

Knife pleats are folds of fabric that all lie in the same direction. They may be used in small numbers or for an entire part of a garment. They may be sharply creased or gently folded, depending on the style required, and may be stitched down or left to hang free. Use two knife pleats facing towards the side seams for the fronts of slacks or skirts, or make a kilt-style skirt with knife pleats all around. Pleats may be sewn down with edge stitching or pressed as sharp folds. Use a pressing cloth when ironing the pleats to protect the garment's surface. Practise marking, pressing, and sewing knife pleats.

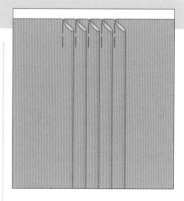

Mark out the pleats accurately. Tack the top 5 cm (2 in.) of the pleats to hold them in place before attaching the pleats to a waist or yoke, and continue to make up the garment. When stitched in place, remove all tacking and press.

Collars

In most cases, a collar is constructed with an upper or outer layer and an under collar (the collar facing), with an interfacing in between. The interfacing gives body and improves the shape of the collar. Choose suitable interfacing – stiff for a crisp finish and lightweight woven for a softer finish. Symmetry is essential. Transfer the pattern markings accurately. Use and adapt the following method for a classic shirt collar to construct the perfect collar for your designs.

WORKOUT 148: MAKE A TAILORED SHIRT COLLAR

The firmness of the interfacing will determine how tailored or casual the collar will be. The collar fall can be buttoned down, or not, and points can be sharply angled or evenly rounded to a curve.

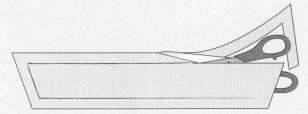

1 For the collar, draw the seam allowance on the outer edges of the stiff collar interfacing. Trim this away, including the pencil line.

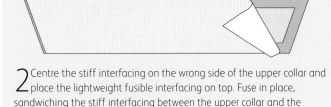

2 Centre the stiff interfacing on the wrong side of the upper collar and place the lightweight fusible interfacing on top. Fuse in place, sandwiching the stiff interfacing between the upper collar and the fusible layer.

3 Place the upper and lower collar (the collar facing) together, with the right sides together. Mark the collar points with a fade-away marker or tailor's tack, then sew along the seam line. Trim the seam allowances; turn through and press flat. Finish with edge stitching.

4 Prepare the stiff interfacing for the collar stand in the same way as above, fusing it to the side that will lie next to the neck.

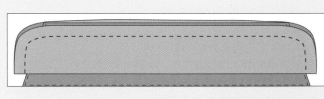

5 Sandwich the collar between the collar stand pieces, matching any pattern-marked notches and dots. Sew these together, layer the seam allowances inside, turn to the right side, and iron for a crisp finish.

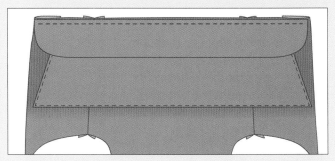

6 Join the outside of the collar stand to the right side of the neck edge and sew together. (Snip into the seam allowance of the neck edge to allow easy matching if necessary.)

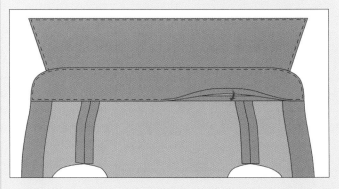

7 Tuck up the seam allowance on the inside of the collar stand and pin in place. Edge stitch through all the layers.

Sleeves

A sleeve that is eased into the shoulder area produces a smooth finish with no tucks or crinkles. The sleeve itself may be short or long, slim-fitting, or flared, but should lie in a simple, flat line where it is attached to the shoulder.

WORKOUT 149: ADD A SLEEVE

Try removing and then inserting a sleeve into an old garment. The trick for a smooth finish is to take time to distribute the tiny gathers of fabric uniformly over the sleeve cap.

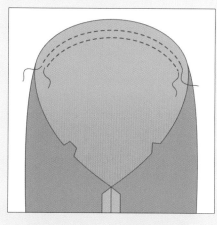

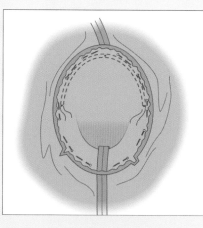

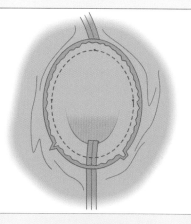

1 Set the sewing machine to the longest straight stitch and sew two parallel lines along the edge of the sleeve cap between the pattern-marking dots, either side of the seam line (or inside the seam line in the case of delicate fabrics).

2 Ease up the gathers and place the sleeve in the armhole with right sides together and raw edges matching. Working from inside the sleeve, match up the pattern notches, dots and seams. Pin along the seam line, distributing the tiny gathers evenly until they disappear.

3 In the pinned state, turn through and check the finished look. Adjust the eased fabric, if necessary, then turn it back again and sew with a standard-length straight stitch.

Check the finished sleeve seam, then neaten the raw edges on the inside with a sewing machine zigzag or other suitable stitch. Trim away the excess fabric.

WORKOUT 150: ADD A GATHERED SLEEVE HEAD

On a gathered sleeve head, clearly defined tucks create fullness along the shoulder seam, or a "puffed" sleeve. This kind of sleeve is easier to insert than an eased-in sleeve (see previous workout). The technique is very similar but the gathers mean there is more room for adjustment. However, it is important to take time to arrange the gathers evenly.

Waistbands

A waistband is added to a skirt or trousers to finish the edge, and it may open at the front, side, or centre back. Waistbands are suitable for all styles of garments that incorporate gathers, darts, tucks, or pleats.

An interfacing is needed to add body to the band and to help it stay in place. Soft perforated interfacings, as well as straight or curved stiff bands, are available in various widths. These can be fused to the wrong side of the fabric or sewn in place. Practise attaching a waistband to an old skirt.

WORKOUT 151: MAKE A WAISTBAND

Always follow the fabric grain when cutting out a waistband. They normally run along the length of the grain. Sometimes, to achieve a particular effect, the fabric can be cut be across the grain. It should not, however, be cut on the bias, since the waistband would not then be stable.

When preparing a waistband, always allow 1.25–2.5 cm (½–1 in.) extra length for comfort. Make sure gathers at the waistline are distributed evenly and that any darts or tucks are positioned correctly before applying the waistband.

1 Cut the waistband to the correct length and width, along with added seam allowances. Mount the interfacing to the wrong side of the fabric.

2 Place the raw edge of the waistband to the waistline edge of the garment, with right sides together. Pin and then machine sew with a straight stitch.

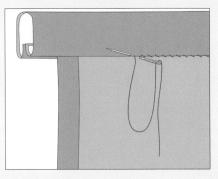

3 Fold the waistband lengthways and press it up and over the waist to conceal the raw edges. Fold the opposite edge under and pin in place, leaving one end extended 1¼ inch (3 cm) for the fasteners. Sew down by machine stitching in the ditch from the outside, or by hand-hemming on the inside.

4 Neaten the ends of the waistband by folding one edge in and slip stitching. On the opposite, longer end, tuck the raw edges in and slip stitch to finish. Sew hooks and eyes or a button and buttonhole in place to finish.

WORKOUT 152: TRY AN ALTERNATIVE WAISTBAND FINISH

Now try this alternative waistband finish. Neaten the raw edge of the waistband with a zigzag stitch and lay flat on the inside without folding under. "Stitch in the ditch" (stitch through the existing seam, as shown by the dotted line on the diagram, right) to secure the waistband.

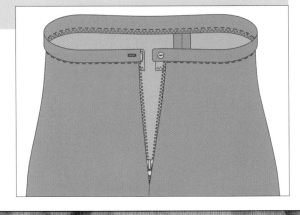

Linings

A lining is constructed separately and sewn in to cover the inside of a garment. It provides a neat finish since it conceals seams and raw edges and also adds body and support to the outer shell, which prolongs the garment's life. The lining fabric can be chosen to add warmth, use a lightweight silk-satin lining to produce a comfortable yet luxurious finish. Choose an appropriate lining for the garment. If the outer fabric can be machine washed, the lining must not be dry clean only. Practise lining on an old straight skirt. You can then move on to other garments.

WORKOUT 153: LINE A SKIRT

Lining a skirt will add body, make it more comfortable, and prolong its life. Any skirt, whether straight, flared, gathered, or pleated, can be lined. As a general rule, the skirt pattern is cut out and made up in lining fabric, then attached at the waist; no separate pattern is needed.

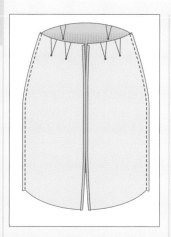

1 Cut out the skirt pieces in lining fabric and sew the skirt lining together, right sides facing. Leave a gap at the zip position and also the back vent if there is one. Mark the dart positions but leave them unsewn.

2 Drop the lining into the skirt with the wrong sides together. Pin at the waist and tuck in the darts, then tack.

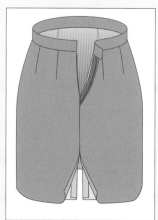

3 Tuck the seam allowance under at the zipper and slip stitch in place. Add the waistband, sewing the skirt and lining as one, and neaten the hem of the lining. Leave the lining back vent open; just neaten the raw edges.

WORKOUT 154: LINE OTHER GARMENTS

Pleated skirt
Cut out the lining of a pleated skirt minus the pleats. Instead, join it with a seam and leave it open behind the pleats to allow for stride width. Making up the lining with pleats would only add bulk to the skirt.

Full gathered skirt
Cut the lining for a full gathered skirt in an A-line style and join at the waist as described above. There is no need to add unnecessary bulk with extra gathers, and there will be plenty of stride room with an A-line shape.

Lining a dress
There are so many dress styles that each design will dictate details on how the lining is to be cut and attached. On the whole, however, if the dress has a waist, the bodice and skirt linings will be cut separately and joined there.

Lining trousers
Ladies' evening trousers may be lined, especially if made in a lightweight and softly draping material. It is more usual to underline tailored trousers at the front just down to the knee. This helps to prolong the wear of the garment.

Closures

Fasteners or closures include zips, buttons, hooks and eyes. They come in various sizes and weights and can be sewn in place or secured to fabric with special clamping tools. Some are purely functional while others are elaborate and decorative.

WORKOUT 155: INSERT A CENTRED ZIPPER

This method places the zip teeth in the middle of a seam. It's an easy technique ideal for beginners. A 2.5 cm (1 in.) seam allowance is used.
This makes it easier to insert a zipper.

 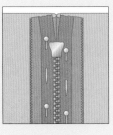 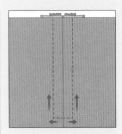

1 Make a plain seam 1.5–2.5 cm (⅝–1 in.) where the zip is to be placed, leaving the zip length open.

2 With the longest straight stitch on your machine, complete the seam. Don't finish the thread ends – these are temporary.

3 Press the seam open, and with the wrong side facing up, place the zip face down with the teeth over the seam. Pin both sides.

4 Tack the zip in place and stitch from the right side of the garment. Start from the bottom and sew to the top each time. Remove all the temporary stitches.

WORKOUT 156: SEW ON BUTTONS

When sewing on a button with holes, make a thread shank (see below) to accommodate the buttonhole's depth. Use strong thread and attach buttons to a double thickness of fabric. In the case of large buttons, sew a small plain one behind the larger one on the wrong side of the fabric to anchor it. For a button with a shank sew as below, but take the needle directly through the shank without leaving the threads slack.

Buttons with holes

  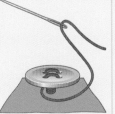 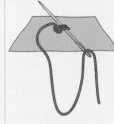

1 Secure the thread end in the fabric and take the needle up through one hole.

2 Take the needle back down through another hole and into the fabric leaving the thread loose, that is, keeping the button and fabric apart. Use a matchstick to help if necessary.

3 Make several stitches, as above, and bring the needle out between the button and fabric. Wind it around the loose central threads a few times to create a shank.

4 Take the needle through to the wrong side and loop through the threads to tie them together. Secure the thread end.

WORKOUT 157: SEW BUTTONHOLES

Many modern sewing machines offer a large selection of preprogrammed buttonholes to suit different types of fabric and styles of garment. Even basic sewing machines have a four-step or a one-step automatic buttonhole setting. Find out about the buttonhole settings available on your machine and try some of them out. You can also hand-sew buttonholes by working around the edge of the opening using buttonhole stitch (see workout 158).

WORKOUT 158: SEW ON HOOKS AND EYES

Hooks and eyes
Hooks and eyes are used as fastenings where edges meet, at the top of a zip, for example.

Hooks and bars
Hooks and bars are for edges that overlap, as on a waistband. Sew them on using the same method as for hooks and eyes.

Snap fasteners
You can also attach snaps using buttonhole stitch.

Sewing on hooks and eyes

1 Place the hook and the eye to allow the two edges to meet and lie flat.

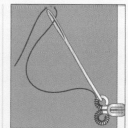

2 Work around the metal with buttonhole stitches to hold both the hook and the eye securely to the fabric.

Buttonhole stitch

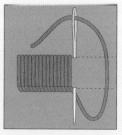

Buttonhole stitch is made by placing parallel stitches very close together as shown above.

▨ Elastic

Elastic can be sewn directly into a garment or threaded through a channel or casing. It allows clothes to be pulled on and off easily.

WORKOUT 159: CREATE A CASING

The traditional way to elasticize an edge is to create a casing and then thread elastic through it. This allows the elastic to be adjusted easily – ideal for cuffs and waists.

1 Sew the garment seams. It's easier to work with a continuous length – this will also give a neater finish.

2 Press the edge of the fabric under 6 mm (¼ in.) to the wrong side. Press the edge under again, this time the width of the elastic plus 3 mm (⅛ in.). Pin in place.

3 With a straight stitch, sew the folded edge of the casing down. Sew over the first four stitches with the last four to secure the threads. Repeat around the top edge.

4 Remove the stitches from the seam and thread elastic through the casing. Adjust the length and secure the ends of the elastic and seam.

WORKOUT 160: ATTACH ELASTIC

Alternatively, stitch elastic directly to the fabric. Quarter pinning is a useful technique for preparing elastic to be stitched in place. It allows the gathers to be evenly distributed.

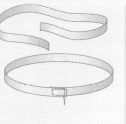

1 Cut the elastic to the correct length and lap and sew the ends together. Make up the seams in the garment to produce a continuous length of fabric to be elasticized.

2 Divide and mark the elastic into four equal parts and do the same with the garment piece – do this at the waist edge, for example.

3 Match up the quarters of the elastic and the garment and pin together.

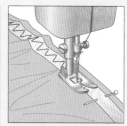

4 Stitch together. Use a narrow stitch for wide elastic or a three-step zigzag for narrower elastic, pulling the elastic to the length of the fabric as you sew. Work from pin to pin to attach elastic evenly.

Pocket workouts

Set yourself a challenge

These workouts are designed to make you think about fashion design. You can use them to build on the skills you have learned throughout the rest of the book, or they might get you interested in a new area of fashion. Whenever you have some spare time, have a look through and pick one of these bite-sized challenges.

161 Design outfits for a band of your choice. You can reinvent them as a different genre or enhance their existing look. You could extend this by designing both stage costumes and more everyday clothes for them.

164 Design a range of clothing to coordinate with an accessory you have seen in your most recent style magazine. Think about the customer who would buy the accessory you have chosen as your starting point and make sure the clothing will appeal to them.

166 Research a particular era that interests you, such as the Sixties or Seventies, or even the 1920s or 19th century. Draw a collection, using fabrics that you have tried to match to the originals, based on this research. Try to link your research to specific designers, such as Mary Quant, John Bates, and Courrèges for the Sixties; and Halston and Biba for the Seventies, for example.

162 Design a "red carpet" dress for a celebrity of your choice. You may want to do some research into vintage couture dresses for this task.

163 Design a range of accessories to match one of the outfits or collections you have designed. By accessories we are usually talking about bags, jewellery, and belts. You can also think about hats, shoes, and gloves in this category. Think about motifs and colour stories.

165 Design a denim collection. This should include jeans and jackets as well as skirts. A denim range should include lots of details specific to that genre, such as interesting washes and distressing, stitch details, pocket designs, special fastenings, and labels. You may also want to include some different items such as simple jersey T-shirts.

167 Design a sportswear range. Sportswear may be performance wear, designed to enhance an athlete's performance through innovative, hi-tech fabrics and finishes. Or it may be more casual for everyday comfort.

168 Design a beach or swimwear wardrobe. This is a good opportunity to think about using colour and printed textiles if you don't normally do so. You might want to include accessories.

169 Design a geometric print range using bold colours and cut-out shapes based on manmade objects or architecture.

170 Design a range of prints based around the natural world. This could be items such as sea shells, pebbles, insects, animals, flowers, or trees, for example.

171 Look at jersey garments, which include T-shirts and many other common items. Produce a range that uses only jersey. You can think about using several sections of different coloured jersey together in one garment. (This is called colour blocking and helps add construction interest.) Oversized T-shirts can provide large samples of jersey fabric inexpensively. This is a good opportunity to try your draping skills as jersey is very fluid and falls nicely.

172 Think about collars all day. Then, in five minutes at the end of the day, see how many you can draw. This will test both your powers of observation and your creativity.

173 Try the previous workout for different types of fastenings.

174 Try workout 172 for types of sleeves.

175 Restyle your best friend. Think about how to change his or her look for everyday and for a specific occasion. Take photos of the results.

176 Treat your mum to a makeover. Give her a complete new look, with ideas for make-up and hair as well as the new outfit you are going to put together for her.

177 Write a news story on what is currently hot in your locale/neighbourhood. If this works out well, see if the local paper will publish it.

178 Design a collection based on a current affairs story. Try to do this in an imaginative and creative manner, not worrying about how you are going to make it and whether it is wearable. Just keep thinking about illustrating the narrative of the story.

179 Research traditional or ethnic costume and design a high-fashion range based on this. When you are doing this, it is useful to look at the work of other designers who are renowned for this approach, such as John Galliano, Dries van Noten, Vivienne Westwood, Alice Temperley, Ralph Lauren, Rifat Ozbek, and Manish Arora, to name a few.

180 Make a garment out of the morning newspaper. Think about strong shapes, cuts, tears, and folds. You can use glue, sticky tape, staples, and other simple joining materials. Remember to photograph the process and your results.

181 Reinvent the wedding dress. Although the traditional wedding dress has its place, it is not a fashion item. How can you make it one? Try using different fabrics, not just silks and satins. You could also experiment with prints and embellishments, contemporary necklines, or the length of the dress.

182 Do something unexpected. A designer needs to be innovative, new and interesting!

183 Go shopping with £20 and buy an outfit with it (including shoes).

184 Take one of the images from your previous research and use it as a styling look. Remember the job of a stylist is to come up with new looks.

185 Take your sketchbook and favourite drawing medium to a crowded area in your school or college. Find a place to stand or sit to one side, out of the way, and see how many people you can draw in five minutes – your sketches should be accurate enough to tell people apart and identify some interesting details about them or their clothing.

186 Make studies of figures but restrict yourself to using only circles. Think particularly about the musculature of people's bodies and the rounded female form.

187 Design a range using only circular or square shapes. Think about what the garments would look like from above, from the side, and from underneath. Also consider how you can incorporate as many circles and squares as possible. Think about silhouette and how basic shapes will respond when constructed using different fabrics.

188 Design a range for your favourite designer. You could choose to concentrate on just one area, such as knitwear or coats.

189 Invent a title and concept for your own indie fashion magazine. You might want to look through your collection of fashion magazines and think about what it is you want to do better or different.

190 Using the Internet for research, write an editorial on the new collections that come out around February and September each year. Consider the differences between the major fashion centres of Paris, Milan, New York, and London.

191 Identify four different key looks from the runway this season. You can put these together from photographic imagery.

193 Illustrate the four different looks that you identified in the previous workout in an appropriate illustrative style. You can use different media for your work, such as collage, watercolour, or pen and ink.

194 Style a photo shoot around one of the key looks from the runway that you have identified. Think about themes, hair, make-up, location, props, and how you want to present the garments.

195 Translate your own personal logo, tag, or brand into appliqué. Apply it to a basic T-shirt. You can use any type of fabric or fabrics (print works well) for the appliqué. You can also stitch the appliqué on with contrasting coloured thread.

196 Translate a menswear range into womenswear. Think about the different body shapes.

197 Translate a womenswear range into menswear.

198 Visit a store that sells clothing and ask which the best-selling items are. Look at how and where they are displayed in the store. Make notes on this merchandising information.

192 **Design a coat and from this develop the rest of your range. The coat is usually the key piece in a fall/winter range. It should define the overall look and silhouette of the collection to follow.**

199 Try to identify the different looks or themed stories in a clothes store. Make notes about what you discover.

200 Design a range using stripes of different colours and sizes. You can repeat the exercise using spots and checks.

201 Choose a children's story and illustrate it using your own designs for the characters and locations.

202 Design an outfit to advertise an existing product, brand, or service. You could take the opportunity to explore your graphics skills by redesigning the company logo. Some very famous designers have worked in this area, particularly for airlines.

203 Make a very quick outfit to go out in. Limit the time allowed for this task to just a couple of hours.

204 Look back over the work you have built up and reflect on it. Write a list of your strengths and weaknesses, what you enjoy, and what you don't. This evaluation should help you realize which area of the fashion industry you would ultimately like to go into. You may also want to do some research into careers in fashion at this point.

205 If you want to go to college, it's a good idea to visit some places that offer the course you're interested in. Try and talk to some students already on the

206 **Take photos of your favourite window displays. You may also want to collect information on this by browsing the larger and designer stores' Web sites.**

course. Each course has its own distinct flavour, and it's important that you choose the one that is right for you.

207 Immerse yourself in fashion. Subscribe to one of the younger and more directional magazines – you should be able to discover them on the Internet. You should also look at *Vogue Italia* regularly.

208 **If you haven't done so already, enrol for a life drawing class – and even if you have, do it again! Understanding fashion is all about understanding the human body.**

209 Get some work experience. This can be added to your CV when you leave school and will be invaluable for impressing potential employers. It is easier to get experience in fashion in some places than in others, but fashion is a huge field, and most creative jobs will have some relevance to what you intend to do.

210 Remember never to take yourself too seriously. Even if you do all the tasks in the book, you may not be recognized as being the height of fashion. This is to do with being in the right place at the right time. Just do your best to be there, and work hard.

Resources

The following list comprises only a very small selection of the many colleges and universities worldwide with departments of fashion design. Whether you are looking for an evening class or for a full-time course in an undergraduate or postgraduate degree programme, there is a huge variety of options available.

U.K.

University of Brighton
Brighton BN2 4AT
t.: (+44) (0)1273 600 900
www.brighton.ac.uk

Central St Martin's College of Art and Design
London WC2H 0DU
t.: (+44) (0)20 7514 7000
www.csm.arts.ac.uk

De Montfort University
Leicester LE1 9BH
t.: (+44) (0)116 255 1551
www.dmu.ac.uk

East London University
London E16 2RD
t.: (+44) (0)20 8223 3405
www.uel.ac.uk

Kingston University
Surrey KT1 1LQ
t.: (+44) (0)20 8547 2000
www.kingston.ac.uk

London College of Fashion
London W1G 0BJ
t.: (+44) (0)20 7514 7344
www.fashion.arts.ac.uk

University of Manchester Institute of Science and Technology
Manchester M60 1QD
t.: (+44) (0)161 236 3311
www.manchester.ac.uk

Middlesex University
Cat Hill Campus
Herts, EN4 8HT
t.: (+44) (0)20 8411 5555
www.mdx.ac.uk

Nottingham Trent University
Nottingham NG1 4BU
t.: (+44) (0)115 941 8418
www.ntu.ac.uk

Ravensbourne College of Design and Communication
Kent BR7 5SN
t.: (+44) (0)20 8289 4900
www.ravensbourne.ac.uk

Royal College of Art
London SW7 2EU
t.: (+44) (0)20 7590 4444
www.rca.ac.uk

University College for the Creative Arts
Surry KT18 5BE
t.: (+44) (0)1372 728811
www.ucreative.ac.uk

University of Westminster
Harrow Campus
Harrow HA1 3TP
t.: (+44) (0)7911 5000
www.westminsterfashion.com

University of the West of England
Bristol BS3 2JT
t: (+44) (0)117 32 84716
www.uwe.ac.uk

Australia

Royal Melbourne Institute of Technology
Melbourne, Victoria 3001
t.: (+61) 3 9925 2000
www.rmit.edu.au

Canada

Montreal Superior Fashion School
Montreal, Quebec H3H 2T2
t.: (+1) 514 939 2006
www.collegelasalle.com

Denmark

Copenhagen Academy of Fashion Design
2200 Copenhagen N.
t.: (+45) 33 328 810
www.modeogdesignskolen.dk

France

Creapole
75001 Paris
t.: (+33) 1 4488 2020
www.creapole.fr

Esmod Paris
75009 Paris
t.: (+33) 1 4483 8150
www.esmod.com

Parsons Paris
75015 Paris
t.: (+33) 1 4577 3966
www.parsons-paris.pair.com

Italy

Domus Academy
20143 Milano
t.: (+39) 24241 4001
www.domusacademy.it

Polimoda
I-50143, Firenze
t.: (+39) 55 739 961
www.polimoda.com

Netherlands

Amsterdam Fashion Institute
1091 GC Amsterdam
t.: (+31) 20 592 55 55
www.amfi.hva.nl

Spain

Institucion Artistica de Ense-anza
28001 Madrid
t.: (+34) 91 577 17 28
www.iade.es

U.S.A.

American Intercontinental University (Buckhead)
Atlanta, GA 30326
t.: (+1) 888 591 7888
www.aiubuckhead.com

American Intercontinental University (Los Angeles)
Los Angeles, CA 90066
t.: (+1) 800 421 3775
www.aiula.com

Brooks College of Fashion
Long Beach, CA 90804
t.: (+1) 800 421 3775
www.brookscollege.edu

Cornell University
Ithaca, NY 14853
t.: (+1) 607 254 4636
www.cornell.edu

Fashion Institute of Design and Merchandising
Califonia
www.fidm.com

Fashion Institute of Technology
New York, NY 10001
t.: (+1) 212 217 7999
www.fitnyc.edu

International Academy of Design and Technology (Chicago)
Chicago, IL 60602
t.: (+1) 312 980 9200
www.iadtchicago.edu

Katherine Gibbs School
New York, NY 10138
t.: (+1) 212 867 9300
www.gibbsny.edu

Parsons The New School for Design
New York, NY 10011
t.: (+1) 212 229 8590
www.parsons.edu

School of Fashion Design
Boston, MA 02116
t.: (+1) 617 536 9343
www.schooloffashiondesign.org

Index

Index

Credits

Key: l=left, m=middle, r=right, t=top, b=bottom

The authors and editors would like to thank and acknowledge the contributing artists for kindly submitting work for inclusion in this book.

- Jenny Ambrose (www.enamore.co.uk) 20l&r, 21l
- Lara Angol 14c, 41mr
- Clare Armstrong 37tl, 71t
- Manish Arora 55tl
- Emma Bergamin-Davys 14l, 23b, 41tl
- Katie Buglass 77r, 85l, 87l,c&r
- Flic Bull 21tr,mr&br
- Gemma Compton 14r
- Cathy Craig 31t, 35tr, 38mr, 70b
- Laura Davy 38b 72–73t
- Poppy Dover 103tr&bl
- Kate Edwards 74–75b
- Rachel Fong 101b, 104tr
- Charlotte Franke 47r, 102tr&m
- Jean Paul Gaultier 36bl
- Gucci 27b, 28br
- Matthew Harding 101t, 103ml&br
- Weiqiong Huang 71b
- Zoe Jeffrey 48l,m&r
- James Jennion 89t
- Alexandra Kaegler 28bl, 36tr, 80b, 81tl
- Sarah Kerridge 54t&b
- Paul Laidler 31c&br
- Christie Li 1, 2l, 3, 4, 5, 39r, 47l, 95r, 128r
- Lily Mason 17bl,bm&br
- Rhian McLaren 34bl
- Dawn Elyse Munro 6bl, 102bl&br, 122bl
- Clover Newman 72b
- Huyen Ly Nguyen 2b&r, 46l&r
- Etienne Ozeki (www.etienneozeki.com) 26b
- Lisa Pearce 52–53all
- Lois Porte 33t,m,bl&br
- Lee Rey-Ient 41bl
- Felipa Rojus 103mr
- Heather Rowan-Robinson 70t
- Leanna Smith 29tr
- Martina Spetlova 94r, 104ml&mr
- Hanna Siobhan Stewart 15br&bl
- Hannah Tamplin 72b
- Shani Van Breulelen 104tl,mml,mmr&b, 105t
- Sarah Waldock 13t&b, 16b, 29tl, 39t, 45l, 47m, 68–69t
- Mary Warren 61tr, 76tr, 93t
- Charlotte Watson 42br
- Debbie Waygood 31bl
- Tamsin Weston 61m&b, 62bl
- Eric Wong 105b
- Charlotte Wood 97t
- Sophie Worgan 55b